76
92

DATE			

DRUG
TESTING

DRUG TESTING

BY GILDA BERGER

AN IMPACT BOOK
FRANKLIN WATTS
NEW YORK/LONDON/TORONTO/SYDNEY/1987

Photographs courtesy of: UPI/Bettmann Newsphotos: pp.
2, 11 and 17 (Reuters), 13, 18, 34, 48, 60, 64, 66, 69, 78, 81,
109, 112; ROTHCO Cartoons: pp. 8 (© Dan Hofoss-Canada),
57 (© Kirk-Toledo Blade, Ohio), 89 and 93 (© Engleman);
DEA: pp. 21, 23, 25, 30; AP/Wide World Photos: p. 39.

Library of Congress Cataloging-in-Publication Data

Berger, Gilda.
  Drug testing.

  (An Impact book)
  Bibliography: p.
  Includes index.
  Summary: Discusses the legal, ethical, and social
issues surrounding the use of drug tests, used by
schools, employers, the government, and sports teams
to diagnose or punish individuals using drugs.
    1. Drug testing—United States.   2. Drug abuse—
United States—Prevention.   [1. Drug testing.
2. Drug abuse]   I. Title.
HV5823.5.U5B47   1987   362.2'9386   87-13369
ISBN 0-531-10411-7

S15576
362.2
BER
88/89
12.90
SHC 88

CONTENTS

DRUG
TESTING

THE
DRUG CRISIS

A WIDESPREAD PROBLEM

The use of illegal drugs in this country is "astonishingly high," says Dr. Donald I. Macdonald, head of the federal Alcohol, Drug Abuse and Mental Health Administration. Drugs are flooding the nation and pervading every aspect of American life. Every year, more than 150 tons of cocaine, 65 tons of marijuana, and 12 tons of heroin spread across the land, from coast to coast, border to border. According to a 1985 government survey,[1] nearly 37 million Americans—about one out of every five people twelve years of age or older—have used one or more illegal drugs.

Illegal drugs, also called illicit drugs or controlled substances, fall into a number of separate groups. They include heroin and other opiates, cocaine and other stimulants (including crack), barbiturates and other depressants, PCP ("angel dust") and other hallucinogens, and marijuana.

Drugs are chemical substances that produce physical, mental, emotional, or behavioral changes in people. The controlled substances are likely to be drugs that are not prescribed but that people take to affect their mood or feeling. Like any drugs that are used for nonmedical purposes, these substances can harm a person's health and well-being. In addition to causing psychological and often physical dependence, illegal drug use often results in diseases, disabilities, and deaths that far exceed the toll of any other illness—indeed, of most other illnesses combined! Between 1981 and 1985, as just one example, cocaine-related deaths in twenty-five major metropolitan centers more than doubled and cocaine-related emergency-room visits tripled.[2]

Apart from the personal tragedies of drug users, much of the crime and violence in our towns and cities comes from widespread drug abuse and users' needs for money to support their drug habits. Sales of illegal narcotics top $100 billion a year. That is more than the total annual income of General Motors—or of all America's farmers.

A recent justice department report showed that heroin addicts commit at least 100,000 burglaries, robberies, and auto thefts every single day. That constitutes about 20 percent of all property crimes. If we add to that total property crimes committed by other addicts, we can probably double the number, according to Joseph A. Califano, Jr., former secretary of the Department of Health, Education and Welfare (now Health and Human Services).

Employers are well aware that between 5 and 13 percent of the work force uses drugs. And they know what this costs their companies in added expenses and production losses. A study done in 1985 by the Research Triangle Institute in North Carolina showed that drug abuse costs American society $47 billion annually, including about $27 billion in lost worker productivity.[3]

*Australian customs officials
examining heroin packages seized
in a $45 million Sydney waterfront
haul in June 1983. Australia is
a transit point for rerouting drugs.*

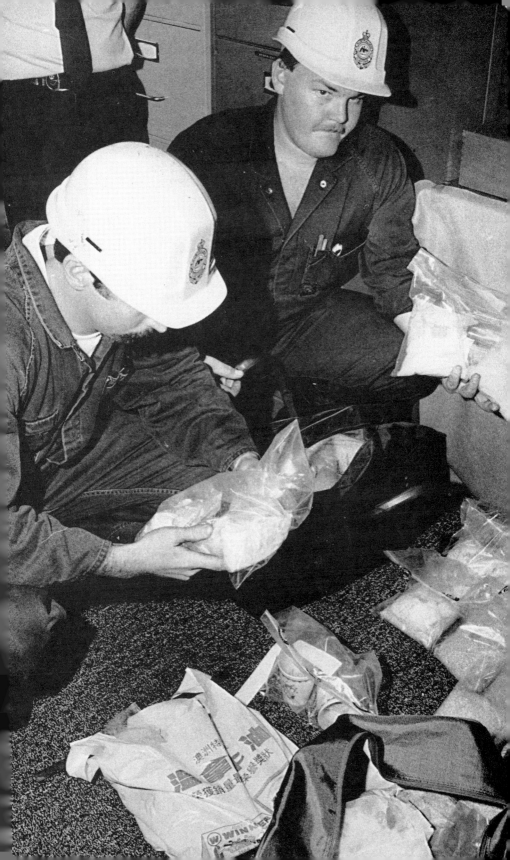

Everyone agrees that the problem of drug abuse in the United States is great. And many believe that something should be done to curb the abuse of drugs by young and old alike. Federal and local drug enforcers have attempted to contain drugs in various ways. But even they admit that their best efforts have not succeeded. Therefore, it is not surprising that people have begun to look elsewhere for solutions.

Some think that a massive effort to test for drugs in schools, workplaces, and locker rooms would be an effective and legitimate way to stem the tide of drug abuse. By the summer of 1986, calls for speedy action against drug abuse had reached a fever pitch. In sports alone, Baseball Commissioner Peter Ueberroth and National Football League Commissioner Pete Rozelle both suggested that the professional players in their sports be required to take drug tests.

But many others seriously question the concept of widespread drug testing on legal and moral grounds. Testing has also been challenged as an impractical and unworkable way to reduce the drug-abuse problem. While the debate goes on, though, the practice of widespread drug testing grows.

THE DRUG-TESTING
PHENOMENON

The increased concern about drug abuse has, in part, been the result of the early 1986 appearance on the streets of crack—a new, powerfully addictive form of cocaine—and the growth of cocaine addiction. President Ronald Reagan warned that "drugs are menacing our society." His administration called for a "national crusade" against drug abuse.

President Reagan, with Vice President Bush looking on, signs legislation that increases federal spending to fight drug abuse and toughens drug laws and penalties.

IT CAN BE DONE

On October 27, 1986, the president signed into law a $1.7 billion antidrug bill. This legislation authorized stricter enforcement of existing drug laws, approved tougher penalties for various drug crimes, and increased the power of police officers to search and arrest individuals for drug use. In addition, Reagan instructed cabinet officers and department heads to begin devising a system of mandatory drug testing for the 2.8 million civilian federal employees who work in sensitive jobs.

The theory of how drug testing will help curb drug abuse is simple. If people know that they will have to pass a urine test to get or keep a job, stay in school, play on a big-league team, or whatever, they will be less likely to experiment with drugs. In addition, those who need help will be found out and directed to appropriate treatment programs. Massive testing is thought by some to be a much better deterrent to drug abuse than the remote possibility of being caught buying or using drugs and going to jail.

Drug testing is already a fact of life in the United States. At least one-third of the largest U.S. corporations tested job applicants for drug use in 1986. Some firms also require on-the-job testing of employees suspected of using drugs. And testing is being used in occupations in which drug-impaired judgment could affect public safety or national security, such as airplane pilots, train operators, air-traffic controllers, police officers, and military personnel.

Still, not everyone accepts drug testing. Even those who agree that some testing makes sense are very undecided about related issues, such as: Is testing legal if there is no reasonable suspicion of drug use? Can testing produce the desired results? When is it justified? Is the deterrent effect worth the loss of privacy?

Before considering these issues, among others, let's take a look at the "target" drugs of the testing programs.

2

THE ILLICIT DRUGS

The abuse of drugs in today's world has been compared to the spread of the plague during the Middle Ages. The latest National Institute on Drug Abuse report on drug use in 1985[4] showed the following:

- An estimated 500,000 in the United States are hard-core heroin users.
- Nearly 5.8 million people use cocaine at least monthly; 20 to 24 million have tried cocaine one or more times.
- Six million people reported that they use marijuana almost every day. One in six employed Americans twenty to forty years of age said they smoked marijuana at least once a month.
- About 1.6 percent of young adults, aged eighteen to twenty-five, said they used hallucinogenic drugs at least monthly.
- About 1.6 percent of the young adult group also reported the illegal use of sedatives, such as barbiturates.

Research shows that drugs are now cheaper, purer, and far more plentiful than ever before. This has boosted the rates of addiction and death from overdoses. Advocates of drug testing hope that testing will help to check the use of the most common illicit drugs that ruin, waste, or cut short people's lives.

HEROIN AND
OTHER OPIATES

Heroin is an opiate. Opiates, which are sometimes called narcotics, are a group of drugs that are used medically to relieve pain.

Some illicit opiates, such as heroin and opium, come from the resin of the Asian poppy plant. Other opiates, such as meperidine (Demerol), are synthesized in laboratories or factories.

Heroin (also called "junk" or "smack") accounts for 90 percent of the opiate abuse in the United States. Heroin is usually a white or brownish powder. Most often, users dissolve the powder in water and inject it into a blood vessel. Street preparations of heroin are frequently diluted, or "cut," with other substances, such as sugar or quinine.

Heroin use has not increased significantly over the past decade. But experts worry about new forms of the drug, such as "black tar," which is up to 99 percent pure, and "China white," a synthetic form of heroin. Such drugs may be responsible for the recent rise in deaths from heroin overdose. Also, doctors fear the new trend toward smoking heroin. This way of using heroin, which is just as dangerous as injecting it and which makes needles unnecessary, may add to its popularity.

A Mexican soldier from
an antidrug brigade
collects illegal poppy
plants for the government.

Also abused are opiates with legal medical use. They include morphine, meperidine, paregoric (which contains opium), and cough syrups that contain codeine. These opiates come in a variety of forms, including capsules, tablets, syrups, solutions, and suppositories.

Opiates tend to relax the user. People who use opiates describe an immediate "rush" of good feelings. But sometimes the user develops bad reactions, including restlessness, nausea, vomiting, and even death.

Occasionally, the drug makes users go "on the nod." This means that they get very drowsy and doze on and off. With very large doses, users may fall into a very deep sleep. Their skin becomes cold, moist, and bluish in color. Their breathing slows down. In the worst cases, death follows.

If individuals take large doses of an opiate or use it occasionally over a long period of time, they will likely become dependent on the drug. For such people, drugs become the main focus in life. The more of the drug they take, the more of it they need to get the same effects and the more dependent they become on having a steady supply of the drug.

The physical dangers to the body depend on the specific opiate used, the dose taken, and the way it is taken. Most of the bad physical results come from overdosing, or taking too much of a drug; from using unsterilized needles; from impurities in the drug itself; or from combining the drug with other substances. Over time, opiate users may develop infections of the heart lining and valves, skin abscesses, and congested lungs. Infections from unsterilized needles can also lead to such serious illnesses as AIDS (acquired immune deficiency syndrome), tetanus, or serum hepatitis.

Over 28 pounds (12.7 kg)
of brown Mexican heroin,
valued at $13 million, in
one suitcase

When those who are dependent on an opiate stop taking it, they usually begin to experience withdrawal symptoms within four to six hours of the last dose. Uneasiness, diarrhea, abdominal cramps, chills, sweating, nausea, and runny nose and eyes are some of the symptoms of withdrawal. Their intensity depends on how much of the drug was taken, how often, and for how long.

Withdrawal symptoms for most opiates reach their worst level approximately twenty-four to seventy-two hours after they begin. They usually diminish within seven to ten days. But symptoms such as sleeplessness and drug craving have been known to last for longer periods of time.

COCAINE AND CRACK

Cocaine is a drug that is extracted from the leaves of the coca plant, which grows in South America. A central nervous system stimulant, cocaine appears in several different forms. Cocaine hydrochloride, which is the most readily available form of the drug, is usually a fine white crystallike powder; it is sniffed or snorted into the nose but can also be injected. On the street, it is known as "coke" or "snow."

When cocaine is snorted, the effects are felt within a few minutes, peak in about fifteen to twenty minutes, and disappear within an hour. The feelings produced include a sense of well-being and a surge of great energy and alertness. There are also physical reactions; among them are dilated pupils and an increase in blood pressure, heart rate, breathing rate, and body temperature.

Crack is a purified, smokable form of cocaine that is especially potent and addictive. Smoking crack produces a shorter and more intense "high" than any other way of using the drug. That is because smoking is the most direct and rapid way to get the drug to the brain. Since larger amounts reach the brain more quickly, smoking crack also increases the basic risks of using cocaine. These dangers include confusion, slurred speech, anxiety, serious psychological problems, and possible death.

Cocaine in its powder form

Even before crack emerged as a popular drug in 1986, 44 percent of cocaine users seventeen years of age or younger reported that they had smoked cocaine in some form at least once. Only half as many people eighteen or older had smoked the drug.

The dangers of cocaine use vary. Some regular users suffer from restlessness, irritability, anxiety, and sleeplessness. Even low doses of cocaine may upset some people emotionally and psychologically. Those who take high doses of cocaine over an extended period of time may become paranoid—feel that others are plotting against them. Hallucinations can also occur, in which people see, hear, or feel things that do not exist.

Cocaine is a dependence-producing drug. After a while, users usually begin to center their lives on getting and taking the drug. Smoking crack increases the risk of this dependence. Often those who have been using the drug over a period of time continue its use just to avoid the depression and fatigue they would suffer if they stopped.

AMPHETAMINES

Amphetamines are also called "speed," "uppers," "dexies," or "bennies." In their pure form, they are yellowish crystals, but they are usually manufactured in tablet or capsule form. Users either sniff the powdered crystals or make a solution that they use for injections. Amphetamines are stimulants. They provide users with a powerful burst of energy.

Amphetamines increase the heart and breathing rates and blood pressure. They also dilate the pupils and decrease the appetite. In addition, the user may experience a dry mouth, sweating, headache, blurred vision, dizziness, sleeplessness, and anxiety. Extremely high doses can cause people to flush or become pale. They may even cause a rapid or irregular heartbeat, tremors, loss of coordination, and physical collapse. An amphetamine injection creates a sudden increase in blood pressure that can lead to death from a stroke, a very high fever, or heart failure.

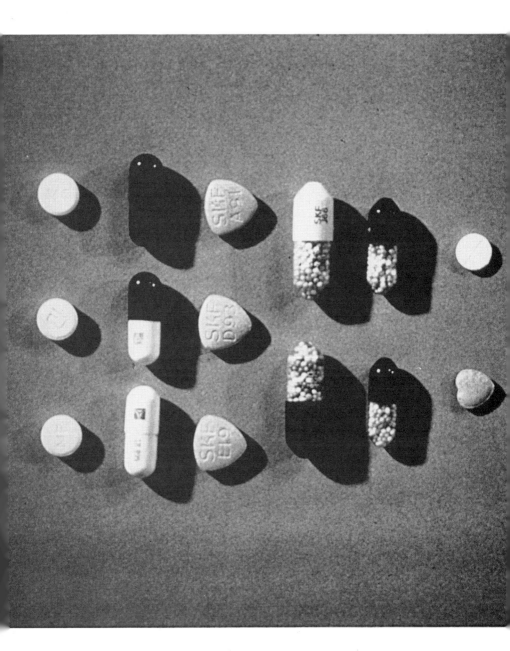

Amphetamines in both tablet and capsule form

In addition to the physical effects of amphetamines, users report feeling restless, anxious, and moody. Higher doses intensify the effects, so that the user becomes excited and talkative, with a false sense of self-confidence and power.

Individuals who take large amounts of amphetamines over time may also develop a so-called amphetamine psychosis. They experience hallucinations, paranoia, and delusions, which are irrational thoughts and beliefs. Bizarre—and sometimes violent—behavior may occur in this state.

Frequent use of large amounts of amphetamines can produce permanent brain damage, resulting in disturbances of speech and thought. In addition, users who inject amphetamines intravenously are liable to get seriously ill from using contaminated needles or solutions. They may fall victim to any of several different kinds of kidney, lung, or heart disease, strokes, as well as potentially fatal blood vessel diseases.

Some people become dependent on amphetamines, feeling that the drug is essential to their normal functioning. These users continue using amphetamines just to avoid the "down" mood they get when the drug's effects wear off.

When amphetamine use is stopped abruptly, the drug user may experience extreme fatigue, sleepiness, irritability, hunger, or depression. The length and severity of the depression seems to be related to how much and how often amphetamines had been taken.

MARIJUANA

Marijuana (also known as "grass," "pot," or "weed") is the common name for a drug made from the plant *Cannabis sativa*. The main mind-altering (psychoactive) ingredient in marijuana is THC (delta-9-tetrahydrocannabinol), but more than 400 other chemicals also are in the plant. A marijuana cigarette ("joint") is made from the dried leaves of the plant. Such cigarettes are often smoked in groups. The "joint" is passed from person to person; each one inhales and holds the smoke in his or her lungs as long as possible for the full effect.

Experiments show that marijuana affects the wide range of skills needed for safe driving. Thinking and reflexes are slowed, making it hard for drivers to respond to sudden, unexpected events in time. The abilities to "track" (stay in the lane) through curves, to brake quickly, and to maintain speed and the proper distance between cars also suffer. Research shows that these skills are impaired for at least four to six hours after smoking a single marijuana cigarette. If a person drinks alcohol along with using marijuana, the risk of an accident greatly increases.

Panic reactions—an extreme fear of "losing control"—may also occur, especially with first-time marijuana users. The symptoms usually disappear in a few hours.

Even though the number of regular marijuana users has declined from 20 million in 1982 to 18.2 million in 1985, 6 million people still use marijuana almost every day. Long-term regular users may become psychologically addicted to marijuana. They have a hard time limiting their use of the drug, they require more of it to get the same effect, and they develop problems with their jobs and personal relationships.

PCP, LSD, AND OTHER HALLUCINOGENS

Hallucinogens are also known as psychedelics and mind-altering substances (though all of the drugs discussed in this book can be considered mind- or mood-altering substances). They change a person's perception, sensation, thinking, self-awareness, and emotions in extreme ways. PCP, LSD, and mescaline are the best-known hallucinogens. They produce hallucinations, as well as the delusions and distortions of time and space that some users find pleasant.

Most often called "angel dust," PCP (phencyclidine) was first developed as an anaesthetic in the 1950s. However, it was taken off the market for human use because of its dangerous side effects—delirium, extreme excitement, and visual disturbances.

PCP is sold on the street as a pure, white powder and as tablets, pills, and crystals. The powder is sometimes mixed with marijuana, parsley or mint leaves, or tobacco. Other times, small cigars called "Shermans" are dipped into a PCP solution and smoked.

Although PCP is illegal, it is easily manufactured in home laboratories. The drug is often sold as mescaline or THC. Sometimes it may not even be PCP but a more dangerous by-product of the drug.

Low doses of PCP produce a floating, euphoric high, sometimes with feelings of numbness. When large doses are taken, the effects include confusion, loss of concentration and memory, difficulty in speaking, and delirium. Very large amounts of PCP can cause convulsions, coma, and even death.

PCP can make normally quiet people behave very violently. Their bizarre behavior sometimes leads to death from drowning, burns, falls (from high places), and automobile accidents. The drug may cause a temporary mental disturbance, called a PCP psychosis, that may last for days or weeks. Long-term abusers of PCP report memory and speech difficulties and hearing voices or sounds that do not exist. Recurring attacks of bizarre, unpredictable, and sometimes dangerous behavior have been seen in some users. The drug remains present in the body for long periods of time.

Users find it difficult to describe or predict the effects of PCP. For some, PCP in small amounts acts as a stimulant; it speeds up bodily functions and changes the way users see their own bodies and the things around them. It alters their speech, muscle coordination, and vision, dulls their senses of touch and pain, and slows down their body movements. Time reportedly seems to move more slowly.

LSD (its scientific name is lysergic acid diethylamide; its street name is "acid") is made synthetically from lysergic acid, which is found in ergot, a fungus that grows on rye and other grains. Discovered in 1938, it is one of the most potent mood-changing chemicals. Just one ounce of the liquid can provide 300,000 average doses! The substance is odorless, colorless, and tasteless. Almost all LSD is illegally manufactured and may contain impurities and adulterants, some quite dangerous.

some abusers of LSD. Symptoms of organic brain damage, such as impaired memory and attention span, mental confusion, and difficulty with abstract thinking, may be strong or subtle. It is not yet known whether such mental changes are permanent or if they disappear when LSD use is stopped.

SEDATIVES

Sedatives are drugs that depress or slow down the body's functions and calm people who are nervous or agitated. They are also called "downers."

Tranquilizers are a type of sedative. Among the best-known tranquilizers are Valium (diazepam) and Librium (chlordiazepoxide). People usually take tranquilizers to relax and to quiet their fears and anxieties.

Minor tranquilizers are the most prescribed drugs in the world, especially for adult women and older men who complain of depression or tension in daily life. These drugs can create the feeling of dependency and are taken too often without real need. For some time it was believed that these were safe drugs, with little danger of overdose or dependency. Now experts say that these tranquilizers do pose risks, including a likelihood of dependency after regular use for six weeks or so and up to ten days of withdrawal symptoms on stopping.

Sleeping pills, or barbiturates, as their name indicates, put people to sleep. In very small amounts, barbiturates can calm nervousness and anxiety. If larger amounts are taken, the drugs promote drowsiness. But at very high doses these drugs may cause unconsciousness and death.

Barbiturates are often called "barbs." In many ways, their effects are similar to the effects of alcohol. Small doses produce calmness and relax muscles. Somewhat larger doses can cause slurred speech, a staggering gait, poor judgment, and slow, uncertain reflexes. These effects make it dangerous to drive a car or operate machinery. Large amounts can cause unconsciousness and death.

Quaalude (or "lude") is the trade name for methaqualone, another type of sedative. Originally prescribed by doctors to reduce anxiety during the day and help patients sleep at night, for a number of years it was a commonly abused drug. Quaaludes also produce effects similar to alcohol's effects. They reduce inhibitions, making users feel free to do things that they would not normally do. As effective pain-killers, "ludes" can also cause physical and psychological dependence. Dangers from abusing Quaalude include injury or death from accidents caused by faulty judgment and drowsiness, and convulsions, coma, and death from overdose.

Regular use of sedatives over time may result in a tolerance for the drug, which means that larger and larger doses must be taken to get the same effects. Heavy use may also lead to both physical and psychological dependence. When addicted users suddenly stop taking the drug, they may develop withdrawal symptoms that range from restlessness, insomnia, and anxiety to convulsions and death. Those who are psychologically dependent feel that they must have the drug to carry on their day-to-day lives.

Taken together, sedatives and alcohol can kill. The combination multiplies the effects of each and greatly increases the risk of death.

3

THE DRUG
TESTS

Fire.)
God.

From the White House to the schoolhouse, from the ballpark to the fire station, from the executive suite to the factory floor, men and women—and children, too—in increasing numbers are being asked to submit urine samples to be tested for the presence of illicit drugs. The country, which is reportedly reeling in a crisis of widespread drug abuse, has turned more and more to drug testing as a way of trying to halt the drug epidemic.

What are drug tests? How do they work? Are they effective?

WHAT DRUG TESTS ARE

A drug test is a chemical analysis used to detect the presence of drugs in a small sample of urine (or sometimes blood). The tests are based on the fact that most drugs remain in the user's system for a period of time. According to J. Michael Walsh and Richard L. Hawks of the National Institute on Drug Abuse, traces of cocaine remain for up to three days, and traces of heroin and PCP remain for up to four; although marijuana may remain for

several weeks, it usually stays for about five days. These lengths can be double for long-term, heavy users of the drugs.

Testing urine for drugs is not a new idea. Drug tests have long been conducted by crime laboratories, hospitals, clinics, and other facilities that treat drug addicts. Ever since the Vietnam War, the U.S. military and a few private employers have been using them. Today tests are more widely used than ever before in many areas of life, including schools, sports, the military, private industry, and government agencies.

Every drug test starts by collecting a urine sample in a glass or plastic bottle. The sample-taking must be closely monitored because drug abusers have many dodges they can use to avoid detection. The most common trick is to substitute someone else's urine for their own. As a matter of fact, newspapers recently reported that a company in Texas has been selling thousands of sealed plastic containers of guaranteed drug-free urine to eager customers!

Fearful test-takers have also been known to dilute the sample by drinking huge amounts of water. Others have taken long drinks of lemon juice or vinegar, and still others have added salt or Drano to their urine to try to throw off the results.

Many efforts have been made to discourage tampering. Sometimes the samples are collected in bathrooms in which the toilet water has been dyed and the faucets shut off. Dr. Robert Newman, president of Beth Israel Hospital in New York, says that a trusted worker "must watch each person urinate into a bottle." He says, "If that is not done, it's a sham."

From the moment it is taken and labeled until the test is completed, each sample must be carefully guarded. This is known as "the chain of custody." A single moment of carelessness, when someone could tamper with a sample or its iden-

*Two chemists analyze molecules
in the blood to determine if a
person recently smoked marijuana.*

tifying papers—in collecting the sample, transporting it to the lab, running the actual test, or preparing the result—can completely invalidate the results.

Laboratory scientists have a number of ways to test urine samples for the presence of drugs. Basically, the tests use one of four methods. In scientific language they are called enzyme immunoassay, radioimmunoassay, thin-layer chromatography, and gas chromatography/mass spectrometry.

Enzyme Immunoassay

The enzyme immunoassay, or EIA, is the most commonly used drug testing method. Its name comes from the principle on which the test operates. The best-selling commercial form of this process is EMIT, short for enzyme-multiplied immunoassay technique. The kit is manufactured by the Syva Company of Palo Alto, California.

The testing machine for EMIT has up to ten separate channels. Each channel tests for a different drug. To start, the urine sample is divided into the desired number of parts to be tested for and fed into the individual channels.

The machine adds a compound made up of two substances to each channel. The first substance is an antibody that is specifically designed to react with a particular drug molecule. The other is an enzyme that causes color change when it is freed from the antibody. If traces of a drug are in the urine, the antibody reacts with the drug and releases the enzyme. If no trace of the drug is present, the enzyme is not freed and the color of the urine does not change.

After the reaction takes place, a narrow beam of light is passed through the urine sample. The light falls on a phototube that measures the color, or wavelength, of the light that emerges from the sample and in this way identifies the drug.

EMIT tests are cheap and fast. They cost only a few dollars per drug tested. A single machine can run up to 500 tests a day.

Radioimmunoassay

Very similar to the EIA is the radioimmunoassay, or RIA. Like the EIA, the RIA machine adds antibodies to the urine that are specific to the target drug. These added antibodies attach themselves to any drug molecules that are present.

The antibodies are "tagged" with radioactive molecules. Such molecules continually send out tiny particles and rays in a process known as radioactivity. The antibodies, with their attached radioactive molecules, are like bells hung around a cat's neck. Wherever the antibody and molecule go (the cat with the bell), they can be found because of their radioactivity (the ringing of the bell).

The test separates all the free antibodies from the sample. If no drugs are present, removing the antibodies eliminates all radioactivity from the sample. But if there are drug molecules in the sample, the radioactive antibodies cling to them, and the sample gives off a low, nondangerous level of radioactivity. This emission of radiation indicates the presence of the drug.

The most widely used RIA test is marketed under the trade name Abuscreen by Roche Diagnostics of Nutley, New Jersey. The biggest customer is the U.S. military, which now prefers the RIA to the other methods. The RIA requires more complex equipment and more training for its technicians than does the EIA. But the Pentagon favors the RIA because it can do more tests, and do them faster, than almost any other approach.

Thin-Layer Chromatography
The process of thin-layer chromatography, or TLC, begins when a glass plate is covered with a thin layer of jellylike substance known as a gel. A small amount of the urine to be tested is applied as a spot near one edge of the gel surface.

The glass plate is then placed upright in a closed container with the edge adjacent to the spot at the bottom. In the base of the container is just enough of a liquid solvent to wet that edge. Bit by bit, the solvent is carried up over the surface of the gel. When the solvent reaches the spot of urine, it pushes all the chemicals contained in the spot up along the surface.

The gel, though, tends to hold on to the different chemicals. The greater the attraction between each individual chemical and the gel, the less it moves. The smaller the attraction, the farther up the glass it moves.

After a period of time, the original spot is gone. Instead, there remains a series of spots, called a chromatogram, going up along the surface of the gel. Each spot is made by a different chemical that has been separated out of the spot of urine.

Scientists have two basic ways to identify the new spots and learn what chemicals or what drugs were in the urine. One method is to spray the spots with chemicals called reagents that are known to produce particular colors when mixed with certain other chemicals. If, for example, a spot turns green when sprayed with a particular reagent, that means there was a trace of cocaine in the urine.

The other method is to compare the chromatogram with spots formed by doing TLC on known chemicals. If a spot from the urine sample comes out in the exact same location as a spot produced by cocaine, that is proof that the urine contained cocaine.

One of the more popular prepared TLC kits is called Toxi-Lab; it is produced by Analytical Systems of Laguna Hills, California.

TLC could be the cheapest drug-testing method. A single test can detect up to forty different drugs in a single urine sample. But the results of TLC are not given in the form of numbers by a measuring machine, as in the EIA and the RIA. Rather, the results depend on the skill and experience of the technician reading the TLC plate. That person must use his or her own judgment to decide which, if any, drugs are present.

Gas Chromatography/
Mass Spectrometry
Even though the EIA, RIA, and TLC are good screening tests, they are subject to error. The only test that claims to be 99.9 percent accurate is gas chromatography/mass spectrometry, or GC/MS.

GC/MS is considered to be as effective in recognizing chemicals as fingerprints are in identifying people. Often it is used to confirm positive results of other tests that have indicated the presence of drugs in the urine. It is the only test that

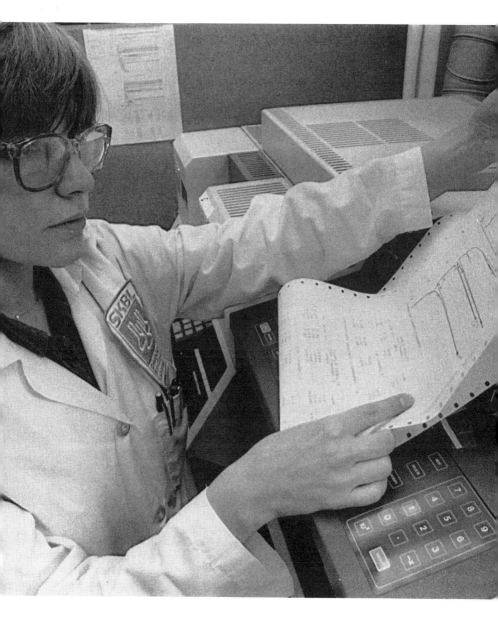

A technician reviews results
from a GC/MS confirmatory test.

is accepted in most courts of law as proof of drug use beyond a reasonable doubt.

The GC/MS machine is a giant $15,000 piece of equipment. It is generally found only in large, well-equipped laboratories and must be operated by highly trained technicians. To run the test, a technician injects a tiny bit of the urine sample into a port in the gas chromatograph. The moving gas carries the sample through a long, narrow tube that is packed with a special chemical. As it passes through the tube, the various molecules in the sample are attracted, strongly or weakly, to the chemical in the tube.

Some molecules are not attracted at all to the chemicals; these pass through the tube very quickly. Others are held very tightly; it takes these a long time to get through. As a result, the various molecules arrive at the end of the tube at different times.

From there the molecules pass into a mass spectrometer. This device ionizes the molecules and sends them through an electromagnetic field that pulls on the individual molecules with varying force, depending on the mass, or weight, and electric charge of each ion. Thus, they are further separated. At the end the machine automatically produces a chart showing exactly which molecules are in the urine sample and the precise amount of each kind of molecule.

The gas chromatography/mass spectrometry test can cost as much as $80 per sample. Besides being expensive, GC/MS is strictly a laboratory tool. It cannot conveniently be used on location in a factory, at an army base, or wherever.

Simple, fast, and reliable new tests for drug abuse are now being developed for on-site use—in doctors' offices, outpatient clinics, offices and factories, and even in the home. These tests, experts say, will produce results in minutes instead of the hours required by current tests. They will also be easier to use, less expensive, and more sensitive than most of today's tests.

Recently a company called Medical Diagnostics introduced a fast, new, inexpensive test. Called KDI Quik Test the machine requires only three minutes to screen for drugs such as morphine, crack, amphetamines, and PCP and can be used anywhere.

Like most of the new tests, the KDI Quick Test uses what is known as a lock and key effect. A drop of urine is placed on a sheet of chemically treated paper. The paper contains antibodies that seek out specific substances found only in the tested-for drug. The antibodies fit the drug molecules like keys into locks. If one or more drugs is present, the test paper changes color.

Quick screening tests, of course, have the advantage of letting larger companies determine inexpensively which employees require further testing. But they could not be used as a basis for taking legal action against employees who test positive for drug abuse. These employees would still have to have the results confirmed by such tests as gas chromatography/mass spectrometry to provide absolute proof of drug use.

DEFECTS OF THE TESTS

Drug tests have become highly controversial. One of the most troubling issues has to do with the results: Are they reliable?

The answer is yes—and no. The scientific theory behind the tests is perfectly sound. But for several reasons the results are occasionally erroneous. That means that people who are completely drug-free can sometimes be accused of taking drugs, and that some drug users are not found out at all.

Manufacturers of the EMIT and the Abuscreen tests claim 99 percent accuracy for their tests. But both warn that every positive test result should be confirmed by another, more elaborate and expensive test method. Since this doubles or triples the cost, such confirmatory tests are not always used.

One important factor in reliability is the quality of the laboratory doing the work. Suppose one person's sample gets mixed up with another's. Or suppose there is sloppy work at the lab, such as a failure to clean the apparatus, so that one sample contaminates another. Such breaks in the chain of custody or human error can cause serious problems.

-41

An example of human error occurred in connection with a December 12, 1986, heavyweight title bout in which Tim Witherspoon was knocked out in the first round by James ("Bonecrusher") Smith. A week after the fight, the New York State Athletic Commission (NYSAC) said that postfight tests of Witherspoon's urine sample had showed traces of marijuana and that the fighter would be suspended. Witherspoon vehemently protested, saying that he had not smoked any marijuana before entering the ring.

A check of the results revealed that someone had made a "critical error" in identifying the specimen. Jose Torres, the NYSAC chairman, explained that the test results, which were negative, were reported as positive due to a clerical mistake. "In order to protect the privacy of the fighter," he said, "we use a code number. Apparently someone in my office misread the number." Witherspoon, it turns out, had not smoked marijuana before the fight.

Many experts express concern about test errors due to faulty lab work. Dr. Bryan S. Finkle, a leading toxicologist at the University of Utah in Salt Lake City, says, "In the climate where there's money to be made, inevitably, there will be incompetent and inadequately staffed laboratories. The tests are very easy to do badly and very difficult to do well."

Dr. Don H. Catlin, chief of clinical pharmacology at the University of California at Los Angeles, says that drug-testing firms "vary tremendously in quality from laboratory to laboratory as well as within the same laboratory on a day-to-day basis." The reason, according to Dr. Catlin, is that "the tests require skill in interpretation, and the reliability of the results depends on who does the test." Dr. Catlin suggests that an effective safeguard for laboratories would be to ask "if the laboratory director is willing to submit an unlabeled sample of his own urine to his own laboratory and then to live or die by the results."

In the spring of 1985, experts at the Centers for Disease Control (CDC) in Atlanta found a high rate of inaccuracy among the nation's drug-testing laboratories. A study of thirteen laboratories serving 262 drug-treatment centers in the United States revealed that all had performed unsatisfactorily and had failed to identify correctly even half of the samples for four out of five drugs tested.

For the CDC investigation, scientists added measured amounts of known drugs to hundreds of specimens of urine. The drugs included barbiturates, amphetamines, cocaine, and morphine. The results varied widely, from zero to 100 percent correct identifications for the various drugs.

Dr. Richard L. Hawks, chief of the research technology branch at the National Institute on Drug Abuse in Rockville, Maryland, says that the technology for detecting drugs in urine "will work, if used properly, but we don't know how often it is used right."

Many of the testing errors concern false positives, in which people are wrongfully accused of having illegal drugs in their urine. Dr. John Morgan, head of the pharmacology department at the City University of New York Medical School, says that drug tests have a false positive rate of close to 20 percent. The problem is that the tests are not always able to distinguish between illegal drugs and chemically similar prescription drugs or foods that are perfectly legal. This is sometimes referred to as *cross reactivity.*

Dr. Morgan has prepared a list of what he calls horror stories of faulty tests. One of the most striking examples involves members of a football team who were tested for drugs using EMIT. Of the hundred players tested, thirty-five tested positive for marijuana. Further study, however, revealed that the players whose test results were positive had taken the popular antiinflammatory pain-killer Ibuprofen. This medicine, which has a chemical formula similar to marijuana's, showed up erroneously in the test as the illegal drug. Improved EMIT tests appear to have corrected this problem.

Another incident described by Dr. Morgan involved a transit worker who ran into trouble because he was taking prescription diet pills that tested the same as Preludin, an abused drug. According to Dr. Morgan, over-the-counter drugs such as Advil and Nuprin, as well as diet pills, can push the rate of error in drug tests even higher than 20 percent.

Neither the EIA nor the RIA can recognize the difference between heroin, a highly addictive and illegal substance, and codeine, a common ingredient in cough syrups and other medications. Both are labeled opiates by these tests, and it is difficult to tell whether the person has taken heroin or codeine. Even more extreme are problems with recognizing amphetamines and PCP, neither of which can be distinguished from similar compounds by the tests. Certain decongestants, diet aids, and prescription drugs can give positive EMIT and RIA test results.

Drinking certain herbal teas may produce a positive test result for cocaine, Dr. Ronald Seigel, a psychopharmacologist at the UCLA School of Medicine, reports. The teas may actually contain very tiny amounts of cocaine. Someone given a urine test after drinking these teas could possibly show a positive result for cocaine.

Dr. Seigel has also written about the many prescription or over-the-counter drugs that contain legal amounts of the barbiturate phenobarbital. A urine test would reveal the presence of barbiturates without identifying the source of the drug. Writer Richard Pollak explains that this may pose problems for workers who must take phenobarbital every day to control the seizures caused by their epilepsy.[5] When tested or forced to reveal their condition, these workers may be unjustly fired, or not hired in the first place. The same may be true for people suffering from depression, diabetes, hypertension, or any of the many other illnesses that millions of Americans keep under control by taking medications.

Even people whose urine actually does contain traces of an illicit drug are not necessarily current users. For example, thirty days after a person stops smoking marijuana, tests may still detect traces of the drug. In theory, someone who sits in a room thick with marijuana smoke may test positive a day later, although this is highly unlikely.[6]

There are also plenty of instances of false negatives, in which people who are on drugs are not uncovered by the test. Sometimes this is due to the unreliability of the test or to an error made in the lab. At other times the sample might contain less of the drug than the minimum standard. The drug could also have been missed because the sample was collected too long after the drug was used or because the sample had deteriorated due to improper storage.

Even the best tests tell only that someone has used the drug being tested for. They don't, in general, tell how much of the drug was taken or when. And perhaps even more important, as Dr. Morgan says, "these tests can tell you nothing about whether the person is impaired."

An extreme example of the difficulty in determining drug impairment is the hallucinogen PCP. Someone can be in a virtual catatonic state from use of the drug and yet test negative for the drug, according to Dr. Seigel. On the other hand, he says, someone else can test positive for PCP and yet show no signs of being influenced by the drug. The reason is that chemicals found in the urine may not be circulating in the bloodstream, where they can affect behavior.

"Testing does only one thing," says Dr. Seigel. "It detects what is being tested. It does not tell us anything about the recency of use. It does not tell us anything about how that person was exposed to the drug. It doesn't even tell us whether it affected performance."

Despite their shortcomings, urine tests are now widely used to detect drug use. The reason is that they are comparatively inexpensive, are accurate if handled properly, and have a long track record—about fifteen years. Apparently, employers and others will continue to use them until a better way is found to curb drug use or until they are outlawed.

4

TESTING
IN SCHOOLS

Item: Student athletes attending high school in the small town of Hawkins, Texas, must take drug tests. So must band members, student council representatives, cheerleaders, and all others involved in extracurricular activities. Those who test positive are not barred from school, but they cannot participate in after-school functions. Extracurricular activities are "a privilege earned," according to the school superintendent.

Item: Since February 1984 a school district in Milton, Wisconsin, has required urine tests of all students who are suspected of drug use and deny it. Students who refuse to submit to the test are suspended from school for three days, and their parents are notified. Students who test positive are referred for treatment.

Item: In August 1985 a high school in Becton, New Jersey, tried to make drug testing part of the complete medical exam required of all high school students. The attempt came after a girl smoked a marijuana cigarette laced with "angel dust" outside the school and nearly died. Under the plan, students who tested positive would not be suspended or expelled but would be placed in treatment.

These are only a few examples of what is happening in U.S. schools today. The controversy over testing young people in school and at home for drugs—and over testing their teachers—is arousing ire on both sides of the issue. On the one hand, school officials are faced with real and immediate dangers caused by student drug use. On the other hand, these officials must also consider the harm done to students by a program that invades a student's privacy.

TESTING STUDENTS

The 1985 report from the National Institute on Drug Abuse (NIDA) reveals a high level of drug abuse among children of school age.[7] The report states, "This nation's high school students and other young adults still show a level of involvement with illicit drugs which is greater than can be found in any other industrialized nation in the world."

School officials claim that ordinary methods of prevention and treatment have not controlled drug use in schools. Many look to the drug testing of students as a way of combating the problem.

Everyone agrees that society has an interest in keeping a proper educational environment in school. Students with drug habits harm both themselves and others. They may disrupt classes and add to a teacher's already difficult job of keeping order.

Since the government requires children to attend school, supporters of testing argue, it must also provide them with a safe and healthy place in which to learn. "Schools have not only a right but a responsibility to insure that the classroom environment is drug-free," says Dr. Robert DuPont, former director of the NIDA.

When the Becton high school decided to make drug testing part of its regular school medical exam, Superintendent Alfred

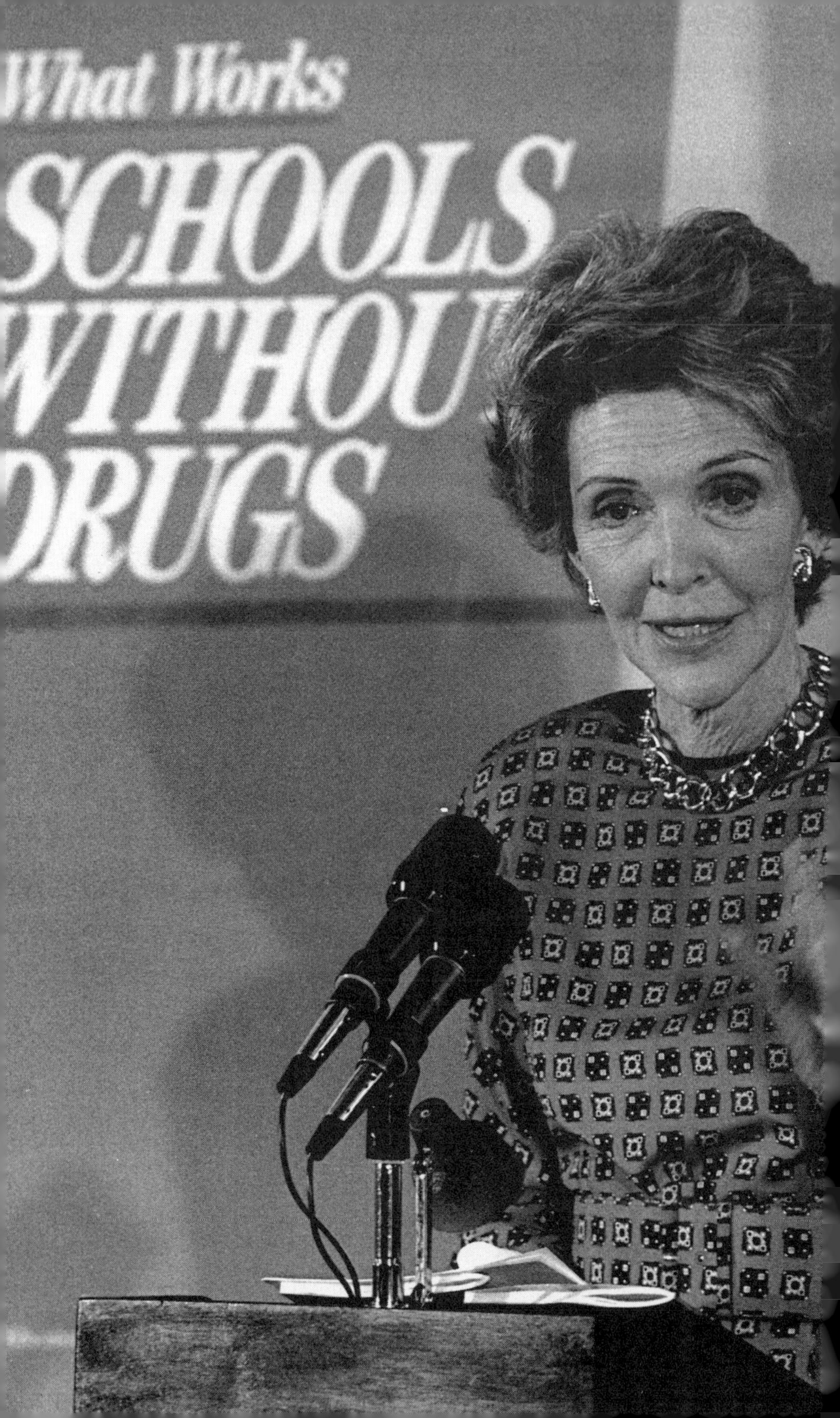
What Works
SCHOOLS
WITHOU
DRUGS

L. Marbaise said, "I feel that, as a responsible person in charge of this school district . . . we have to provide the most safe and educationally conducive atmosphere that we can for our entire student body. . . . When students are involved in an illegal activity . . . they are not only violating their own rights . . . they are beginning to violate the rights of every other student in this school system."

Five students at Becton challenged the policy in the courts. On December 9, 1985, the State Superior Court of New Jersey ruled against Becton's school board.

School officials had to defend their policy of dragnet or blanket testing of *all* students for traces of drugs. They said they considered drug abuse a disease. Just as the school already checks their urine for symptoms of diabetes and other medical conditions, they said, it should also check for drug use.

The American Civil Liberties Union (ACLU) called this argument "obscene." They criticized the concept of using drug testing to "diagnose" drug use. They opposed those who would "permit urine searches to creep into our schools on the coattails of forced medical examinations."

Drug use, the ACLU insists, is not an illness but "plain old criminal conduct." Trying to combat it with "forced medical exams," they say, is "a great intrusion on the individual's privacy." It allows drug users to avoid detection while forcing law-abiding students to submit to degrading urine searches.

Despite what the school officials say, these civil rights experts insist that society treats drug abuse as a criminal problem, not as a medical one. What the Becton school board is really saying, according to the ACLU, is, "Prove that you don't use drugs." In their opinion, this goes against the American

First Lady Nancy Reagan speaks
at a White House gathering of
educators who have successfully
combatted drug use in their schools.

concept that everyone is innocent until proven guilty. It deprives students of due process, the constitutional guarantee of a fair and impartial hearing before being condemned. Even more, it teaches young people to "discount important principles of our government as mere platitudes."

Some school administrators would like to give urine tests only to youngsters whom they suspect of drug use. But many others would give such tests to *all* children within a school, regardless of whether or not they had behaved suspiciously.

The use of urine tests to search for the presence of drugs without regard to a student's behavior has been challenged in the courts. In the 1985 case *Anable v. Ford,* the federal court in the Western District of Arkansas struck down the use of an EMIT drug-screening test on high school students who had been reported to be smoking marijuana in the girls' room. After saying that the test could not tell that a student was under the influence of marijuana while at school, the court stated:

> Certainly it would be beneficial to the vast majority of students who do not use drugs or alcohol, even at home or on the streets, to segregate users from the halls of education. . . . Nonetheless, such conduct is within the realm of parents and law enforcement officials, not teachers and educational administrators. . . . The use of the EMIT immunoassay test, however noble its purpose, reaches beyond the permissible boundaries of school officials.

THE FOURTH AMENDMENT

The chief argument against the practice of blanket drug testing is that it violates the Fourth Amendment, which protects against "unreasonable searches." The Fourth Amendment to the Constitution states that:

> The right of the people to be secure in their persons, houses, papers and effects, against unreason-

able searches and seizures, shall not be violated, and no warrants shall issue, but upon probable cause, supported by oath or affirmation, and particularly describing the place to be searched, and the persons or things to be seized.

The fact is, though, that the Fourth Amendment *only* applies to government searches. It does not legally limit the power of school officials or private employers, except if the principle of fairness—the idea that general searches of innocent people are unfair and unreasonable—is violated.

In 1966 the U.S. Supreme Court ruled that compulsory blood tests are bodily searches. The Fourth Amendment, it said, applied to such searches. A compulsory blood test could be conducted only if there is "a clear indication that in fact . . . evidence will be found." To put it another way, tests can be given to an individual if there is a specific reason to suspect that person of using drugs.

The courts have ruled that every individual has a constitutional right to keep private the personal information contained in his or her bodily fluids. A Georgia court in 1985 (*Allen v. City of Marietta*), felt "constrained by current law to hold that a urinalysis is indeed a search," although it expressed doubt that a urine drug test was the kind of search contemplated by the framers of the Constitution.

The decision to administer a urinalysis without regard to a student's behavior is based on the premise that the individual is a member of a class of people—high school students—known to use drugs. "Drug treatment is fine," says one spokesperson opposed to testing, "if a school has an inkling that a child is involved [in drugs]. But that's very different from doing testing at random."

Giving tests based only on a person's class or society has been called suspicion by association. This notion, some legal experts say, is contrary to the Supreme Court's definition of *reasonable suspicion.* Suspicion of one individual cannot justify a search of other individuals simply because they are similar.

Suppose a certain neighborhood has a high incidence of violent crime. The police cannot defend a blanket search of all residents by claiming that there were many armed individuals among them, they say.

An exception to the Fourth Amendment is the *administrative search*. Border, airport, courthouse, and certain regulated industry searches have all been found to be permissible under the Constitution. Airlines, for example, subject each boarding passenger to a metal detector search of their persons and an X-ray search of their luggage. These so-called administrative searches were instituted to combat hijackers who threatened hundreds of lives and caused millions of dollars in property damage.

Administrative searches have been used in court to try to justify blanket searches in drug-use cases. But federal and state courts have rejected this argument time and time again.

Also, the courts have forbidden searches designed to prevent—in advance—violence, such as that which sometimes occurs at rock concerts. "As unruly as patrons at the Coliseum might have been . . . the dangers posed by these actions are substantially less than those which justified suspending the warrant requirement in courthouse and airport searches." (*Wheaton v. Hagan,* 1977)

School searches for drugs have been judged to be different from airport-type administrative searches. The courts have ruled that the permitted searches take place in voluntary situations. Someone boarding a plane or attending a rock concert may leave instead of submitting to a search. So, too, may a person crossing a border into this country or entering a courtroom as an observer or witness.

Children, however, are required to attend school; they have no choice. A 1985 decision, *Jones v. Latexo Independent School District,* ruled against a program that used dogs to sniff out drugs in the school building. The Eastern District of Texas federal court rejected the analogy to airport searches. In ruling against the program, the judge held that the essential element of voluntary choice was missing.

For blanket drug testing of children in public schools to be legal, experts say, it would have to meet certain conditions:

1. The court must agree that there is a need to search.
2. The court must determine that the search is properly authorized, with safeguards to prevent abuse.
3. The school district would have to show that blanket drug testing would cut drug use and that less drastic methods would not solve the school's drug problem.
4. The drug testing would have to conform to rigorous procedures.

School officials probably could not use a decline in drug use to justify blanket testing. Historically, the courts have not approved dragnet searches to deal with such problems as prostitution and illicit gambling, even though dragnets would almost surely reduce criminal conduct. Searching or testing many to catch a few has always been considered a violation of the Fourth Amendment.

Blanket search programs have also been found by some to have little effect on the problems they are trying to solve. Often they are considered to be merely harassment, shows of power, or "fishing expeditions." Such actions may be considered unreasonable, and therefore unconstitutional. Many feel that blanket testing programs that do not work invite abuse.

Opponents of blanket testing also argue that under our Constitution the government has no right to intrude into our private lives without "probable cause"—that is, without reasonable grounds. A public official demanding a urine sample is just like someone ordering a person to submit to an extraction of blood from his or her body, according to the U.S. Supreme Court. Both violate the Fourth Amendment.

EXCEPTIONS TO THE RULE

Prisons are the only institutions that have the Supreme Court's permission to conduct blanket searches. The decision was set out in the federal case *Storms v. Couglin* tried in New York's Southern District court in 1984. The court said that the constitutional right of prisoners gives way when in conflict with prison security needs. But as Supreme Court Justice Byron White said, "We are not yet ready to hold that the schools and the prisons need be equated for purposes of the Fourth Amendment."

The sole Supreme Court decision about the right to search students in public schools involved a Piscataway, New Jersey, student. In this case, *New Jersey v. T.L.O.* in January 1985, a teacher reported a student found smoking cigarettes in the girls' room. The student was in violation of a school rule permitting smoking in designated areas only. When the girl denied the charge, the assistant vice principal opened the student's purse and spotted a package of rolling papers. Knowing that such papers are often used to make marijuana cigarettes, or "joints," the assistant vice principal thoroughly searched the student's purse and uncovered evidence of drug dealing.

The Supreme Court stated that the Fourth Amendment prohibits unreasonable searches and seizures in public schools. But what is reasonable depends on the context in which a search takes place. Thus, the assistant vice principal was within his rights in searching the purse. Why? He had reasonable grounds to believe that the student had "violated or is violating either the law or the rules of the school." Unlike police, school principals do not need to produce a search warrant. They simply must have "reasonable grounds" for believing that a student broke the law or school rules.

Many experts believe that the courts will continue to allow such searches under the "reasonable under the totality of the circumstances" test. A California court, in fact, recently upheld this kind of search. The case rested on the fact that a student who was found by the dean in the rest room during class without a pass "was nervous or looked nervous."

Perhaps the two sides of the debate over drug testing in schools were presented most clearly by two student leaders at Becton's high school. Sal Incanno, the outgoing president of the senior class, spoke out against the random testing of all students: "If a teacher feels a student is on drugs, he ought to check just that one person." On the other side of the issue, though, was John Donnelly, the incoming president: "I don't mind going through this, if it helps other kids or lets their parents know what's going on."

HOME TESTING

Parents who suspect their children of taking drugs can now test them at home. In July 1986 a home-testing kit called Aware came on the market, put out by American Drug Screens of Dallas, Texas. For $24.95 a parent can buy a urine specimen bottle, a mailing tube, and a lab test. After the youngster provides the urine sample, the parent mails the specimen bottle to the company. Two weeks later, the results arrive in the mail. They tell whether the specimen showed traces of marijuana, cocaine, amphetamines, tranquilizers, barbiturates, or PCP. Positive results come with a note urging the parents to consult a professional for treatment.

Howard Klubeck, who put the Aware kit together, expects to sell tens of thousands of the kits every year. He believes that Aware can be an effective tool in stemming the tide of drug abuse. At the very least, he says, "I think that by bringing that kit into the home, it's going to stimulate some sort of conversation."

Peter True is the president of Kids Saving Kids, a Lancaster, Pennsylvania, organization of teenagers who teach elementary school children about the dangers of drugs. He agrees that opening up family dialogues and getting parents to face the facts of drug abuse are very important. Mothers and fathers often try to ignore signs of drug taking or deny that their child is on drugs. Positive test results, he believes, may convince the parents to seek help.

Lloyd Johnston, a University of Michigan school psychologist and author of the National High School Drug Use Survey, also feels that home testing is beneficial. The threat of a test alone would give kids a good reason to refuse drugs, he says. And refusing drugs in the first place may be the best way to stop drug abuse.

Of course, not everyone believes that testing children at home is a good idea. Dr. Joe Sanders, associate professor of pediatrics at the Medical College of Georgia, suggests that guilty youngsters might doctor up the specimens. If substances were added to the sample, for example, they might throw off the results. He also points out that some drugs may not show up.

As noted above, traces of many drugs disappear from urine after a few days, and positive results do not always mean drugs. The drug company that manufactures Aware claims a 98 percent accuracy rate for its test. In other words, at least two out of every hundred people tested get the wrong results. Either they had used drugs and tested negative or had not used drugs and tested positive.

TEACHER TESTING

Not long ago, and for the first time in the United States, a school district ordered drug testing for teachers. In May 1985, New York State's Patchogue-Medford school district announced that all teachers being considered for tenure would have to take a urine test to make sure they were drug free. School officials said there had been no evidence of drug problems among their teachers. The only justification for the test given by the superintendent was that he had heard rumors that "some teachers were using drugs on social occasions outside of school."

Drug tests are not included in the district's contract with its teachers' union, so the group challenged the policy in court. State health officials argued on the side of the school district. They said that urine tests had been effective with other government employees and that New York courts had upheld the right of police and corrections departments to require them. As the school district's attorney, Robert Sapir, argued, "We don't believe it is an unconstitutional search."

But the teachers' union protested that the district was using "wholesale dragnet tactics" to find out if teachers were using drugs. Representatives of the New York Civil Liberties Union also questioned the test's accuracy.

The school district held that the test for illegal substances is just another health-related test—an addition to the required physical examination. Opponents, though, saw it as a case of what they call "teacher-bashing."

The State Supreme Court, as well as the appellate court, ruled that the school district's plan was unconstitutional. Justice Thomas M. Stark said that the policy was an "impermissible and unconstitutional search of the bodies of the prospective tenured teachers." Thus, the plan would violate the Fourth Amendment, which prohibits unreasonable searches and seizures. Both court decisions made the same basic point: The school district had failed to demonstrate even the slightest suspicion of drug use, which would be necessary to justify such a violation of constitutional rights.

Public opinion is divided on drug testing for teachers. A recent Gallup Poll showed that 64 percent of those interviewed favored the regular testing of teachers for drugs.[8] At the same time, all but one of a large group of members of the New York State Assembly and Senate said they opposed drug testing for teachers.

Few doubt that the problem of drug abuse has invaded our schools as it has other parts of our society. The question is: Are we right in suspending the individual rights of students and teachers in order to try to solve the problem? Or is the blanket testing of groups of people, such as students and teachers, just a "quick fix," perhaps more dangerous than the problem itself?

TESTING IN SPORTS

5

The headlines shout the news:

UNIVERSITY OF MARYLAND BASKETBALL STAR LEN BIAS DIES OF COCAINE OVERDOSE!

DEATH OF CLEVELAND BROWNS' SAFETY DON ROGERS!

ROYALS STAR WILLIE WILSON AND OTHER PLAYERS CONVICTED ON COCAINE-RELATED CHARGES!

GENE (BIG DADDY) LIPSCOMB OF THE BALTIMORE COLTS DEAD OF A HEROIN OVERDOSE!

SIX PLAYERS ON THE NEW ENGLAND PATRIOTS NAMED "ADMITTED DRUG USERS"!

DWIGHT GOODEN TESTS POSITIVE FOR COCAINE!

Amid such reports of athletes on drugs, it is not surprising to learn that the sports world has begun large-scale drug testing.

After the death of Len Bias, the University of Maryland announced a new program that would hold randomly sched-

uled drug tests for every player three times a year. In football, the National Football League (NFL) proposed that all team members have two unannounced drug tests during the season in addition to the one already being given at training camp. In baseball, the commissioner ordered urine tests for players and set penalties for those found to be using drugs. And in tennis, for the first time ever, male competitors at Wimbledon in the summer of 1986 had to submit to drug tests.

Many owners and managers of professional teams consider drugs their number-one enemy. By starting programs of mandatory testing and encouraging treatment for players who test positive as well as imposing penalties on them, they hope to put an end to the growing drug-abuse problem among athletes.

Many of the players themselves, their unions and associations, and civil libertarians position themselves against testing as a violation of human rights. Others have come out in favor of testing—as long as it is linked to rehabilitation and drug education, not punishment.

THE PATRIOTS DRUG SCANDAL

At the 1985 Super Bowl, the New England Patriots were solidly trounced by the Chicago Bears, 46 to 10. That outcome was unexpected. Rumors started flying that the bad plays had been made by impaired members of the Patriots team. Fans raised the question: Did the Patriots lose the game because some of the players were on drugs?

The answer, as it turned out, was negative. But in the investigation some very troubling information did come out. It seems that Raymond Berry, coach of the New England Patri-

New York Mets pitcher Dwight Gooden underwent drug rehabilitation for cocaine use in the spring of 1987.

ots, had known for a year that several of his players had drug problems. However, he had kept his knowledge secret. His justification was that he and the team had "to keep our eye on the bull's-eye." In other words, it was more important to get to the Super Bowl than to help the players who had drug problems.

Soon after that, Patrick Sullivan, general manager of the Patriots, announced the names of six players who were "admitted drug users." According to the team psychiatrist, though, all of them had undergone treatment and were completely drug free at the time of the Super Bowl.

At a meeting after the big game, Coach Berry asked the players to vote for voluntary drug testing. The measure passed by an overwhelming majority. But the NFL Players Association quickly objected. It claimed that the Patriots were bound by collective bargaining agreements that applied to *all* the teams. A single team could not start a testing program on its own.

In any case, the team members withdrew their approval of voluntary testing after Sullivan made his damaging disclosure. The players had assumed that the testing results would be kept confidential. But if there were going to be public announcements of the names of those who tested positive, then they opposed the entire program.

Some civil libertarians have pointed out the dangers of testing players and revealing the names of those who test positive. "People can be tried for revealing business secrets that reduce the value of a commodity," says noted libel lawyer Gerry Spence. "A player is not required by law to give information. If he does under a guarantee of privacy, he enters a contract. If he is named, he could be a victim of breach of contract as well as breach of privacy—and his market value could be reduced."

As for the fans who would resent such action, Spence says, "They forget that a football player's rights are also our rights. Where do they draw the line?"

In January 1986, by a team vote, the New England Patriots decided to adopt their own drug-testing program. The details were developed by themselves and club management. "The guys are taking steps toward getting the team cleaned up," said defensive back Irving Fryar.

MANDATORY TESTING
FOR COLLEGE ATHLETES

In January 1986, the National Collegiate Athletic Association (NCAA) authorized drug testing for athletes competing in the association's championship events and in eighteen post-season college football games. The NCAA agreed to pay 50 percent of the $14,400 cost of testing at the championship events; the other 50 percent would come out of the gross receipts.

The program tests randomly chosen athletes for eighty-six prohibited drugs, including steroids. Steroids are legal prescription drugs that have long been used by athletes to treat injuries but also to improve performance. Although many doubt that steroids make athletes perform better, the drugs can rapidly increase muscle tissue and presumably lead to increased strength and power for athletes.

Steroids are banned in intercollegiate and Olympic competition, but not yet in the National Football League. Those who want to see a ban argue that athletes who use steroids risk damage from liver tumors, heart disease, and sterility.

According to NCAA rules, an athlete found using steroids is barred from competing and is suspended for at least ninety days. Brian Bosworth, an all-American linebacker of the University of Oklahoma was ruled ineligible to play in the 1987 Orange Bowl because a drug test showed the presence of steroids in his body. Bosworth claimed that the steroids he took between January and March in 1986 were prescribed for a shoulder injury. "What I did not know," Bosworth said, "was that the steroids I took would take about a year to clear my body."

Clarence Nunn, a San Diego State cornerback, was not allowed to play in the end-of-the-year 1986 holiday bowl games when the NCAA-mandated drug test he took Christmas Eve came back positive. School officials who investigated said that

the positive findings resulted from a medication that Nunn had bought at the drugstore to treat his flu symptoms. The inhaler apparently contained a substance that is outlawed by the NCAA. Fred Miller, San Diego's athletic director, called Nunn an "innocent victim" of the testing policy. The NCAA said Nunn should have listed the inhaler on the consent form each athlete completes before the drug tests.

Officials of the NCAA see testing as a way of discouraging drug abuse in sports. In the words of Wilford Bailey, the new president of the NCAA: "Our new drug testing program has already had a major impact. . . . We think the NCAA is unique in its position to make an impact on society in this area of great concern."

John Toner, chairman of the NCAA committee on drug testing, says, "Maybe this isn't the perfect answer. But at least we've gotten started. This is a beginning in the right direction for colleges finally facing the seriousness of this problem in dealing with a burning issue in our society."

MANDATORY TESTING FOR PROFESSIONAL ATHLETES

In February 1986, Baseball Commissioner Peter Ueberroth launched a program for testing and disciplining major-league baseball players linked to illegal drug use. Players who tested positive but were not suffering from a severe addiction would be offered counseling and follow-up testing. Team officials did not have to be informed of players' positive results. Players who tested positive and did have a severe drug problem that required long-term rehabilitation, however, would be reported to management.

*John Toner, chairman of the special
NCAA Drug Testing Policy Committee,
announcing plans for drug testing
in all championship games*

Under this plan, seven athletes were suspended for a year. They were then allowed to play again only if they donated 10 percent of their 1986 salaries to a substance-abuse prevention program, agreed to random drug testing, and did two hundred hours of drug-related community service.

Because of rumors that he was involved with drugs, Dwight Gooden, star pitcher for the New York Mets, recently agreed to be tested. The results came back positive for cocaine, and Gooden entered a drug rehabilitation program. Because he went for help, he was permitted to continue to collect on his $1.5 million salary. But Commissioner Ueberroth said, "If the problem arises a second time, we'll take a penalty route."

Columnist Tom Wicker wrote in *The New York Times* on March 11, 1986, that he believes that baseball is forcing some players to give up their legal rights. Young and beginning players, he wrote, are being urged to sign contracts that require random drug tests whether or not they have ever been involved with drugs. He says that Ueberroth is putting baseball's social obligation to provide "role models" for the country's youth ahead of the individual rights of baseball players. According to Wicker, players "ought not to be deprived of citizens' rights, even in the worthy cause of combating drug abuse."

Ira Glasser, executive director of the ACLU, agrees. He says that sports employers who demand general searches of their athletes believe that "if you hang 'em all, you'll get the guilty." In trying to please the public, they are sacrificing the rights and interests of the players. Glasser compares these employers to prosecutors who think it's all right to wiretap without a warrant because people who have nothing to hide should not mind. But the ACLU director believes that people have a right to protect their privacy and their interest against being accused as a result of a mistake.

Baseball Commissioner Peter
Ueberroth explaining his drug
testing plan at a press conference

"Professional sports," writes Glasser, "may indeed provide role models for society. But one of the things that sports employers ought to think about when they talk about role models is the role model they are providing by abandoning fundamental rules of fairness and subjecting innocent and guilty alike to intrusive procedures."

Football Commissioner Pete Rozelle long wanted to take action against drugs in sports. While testifying at a legislative hearing on cocaine abuse in professional sports, Rozelle said that "cocaine . . . in some circles had replaced candy and flowers in the dating process." The problem was made worse, he said, by unscrupulous agents who try to win the right to represent top college stars by offering them cocaine. Carl Eller, former defensive end for the Minnesota Vikings, also testified. Eller told the panel that he used to spend $4,000 a week on cocaine and that it contributed to his early retirement. "I didn't have the quickness. . . . I didn't have the strength," he said.

In July 1986, Pete Rozelle proposed random drug testing of all NFL players. Under Rozelle's plan, there would be two unannounced mandatory urine tests during the regular season. A first-time positive result would bring a minimum thirty-day counseling and testing period. The second infraction would bring a thirty-day suspension at half pay. The third positive test would be punishable by banishment from professional football.

Under Rozelle's policy, the tests would search NFL players for cocaine, marijuana, opiates, PCP, amphetamines, and alcohol. Steroids may later be added to the list of prohibited substances.

Despite the fact that some players approve of testing, the

Gene Upshaw, executive director of the NFL Players Association, talks to reporters after an arbitrator decided players did not have to undergo random drug testing.

NFL Players' Association refused to allow the plan to be "shoved down our throats." Association leader Gene Upshaw said that any testing policy should be worked out by the association and the club owners, not arbitrarily imposed by Commissioner Rozelle.

On November 2, 1986, arbitrator Richard R. Kasher ruled that Commissioner Rozelle had no authority to impose measures exceeding those already stipulated in the players' contract. That contract provides that "there will not be any spot-checking for chemical abuse or dependency by the club or club physician." Under this contract a player can be tested only in preseason physicals or when the club has "reasonable cause" to suspect someone of using drugs.

Meanwhile, some baseball teams are making changes in regard to drug testing. Most members of the Baltimore Orioles, for example, have agreed to a voluntary random testing arrangement operated by the Johns Hopkins Hospital. Team owner Edward Bennett Williams says, "Each has the right not to volunteer without fear of reprisal. We're proud to be in the vanguard." Several other ball clubs are also setting up programs that would link players, not teams, directly to medical facilities in their areas.

Professional sports organizations are clearly moving in the direction of comprehensive drug-prevention and drug-testing programs. Observes John Schuerholz, general manager of the Kansas City Royals, "We are all gravitating toward the same center—and it's about time."

The National Basketball Association (NBA) has no mandatory or random drug-testing programs. But since 1983, in an agreement with its players, the NBA can seek and test when there is "reasonable cause." As David Stern, the league's commissioner, says, "The evidence must be the equivalent of, say, that in which a magistrate would give a sanction for a search warrant or wiretap to law enforcement officials."

Early in January 1987 the NBA got a tip about two players' use of cocaine, Mitchell Wiggins and Lewis Lloyd of the Houston Rockets. Lloyd and Wiggins were ordered to submit to testing. After having tested positive for cocaine, both players were expelled from professional basketball. Both may apply for reinstatement in two years. "Acts like this," Stern stated, "reinforce to people who are abusing drugs or thinking about abusing drugs that there is more reason than ever to say, 'I'll pass.' In high schools, in peer groups, this says, 'It's O.K. to say no.' "

Lloyd and Wiggins are the third and fourth players to be expelled under the drug agreement. Two others, Michael Ray Richardson and John Drew, were prohibited from playing after voluntarily seeking help for drug abuse. Players who freely admit to the use of drugs are given three chances to be rehabilitated. Richardson and Drew had both been given second chances. John Lucas, another player with the Houston Rockets, was dropped by the Rockets for the second time March 14, 1986, after tests showed that he had been using drugs. But he is expected to return to the playing field soon with the Milwaukee Bucks.

THE PLAYERS' HEALTH
AND WELFARE

The discussion of the NFL's drug-testing program brings up a little-talked-about aspect of the drug problem in sports—the innocent victims who might be hurt by drug users during a game. "Our concern," says Commissioner Rozelle, "is the health and welfare of the players—those taking drugs and those injured by those taking drugs."

"We know of numerous cases where a drug user has injured someone else," says Dr. Forest Tennant, Jr., the NFL drug adviser, "some in the NFL, but also in high school and college. If you talk to the team physicians particularly, every one will relate an incident where they believe this has happened."

Although he does not mention specific cases, Dr. Tennant agrees that "spearing"—a player using his helmet as if it were a bowling ball—might sometimes be the result of drug use.

Over the years, the NFL has warned its players that drugs "can cause injury to yourself or to your opponent." But the situation came to a head recently when Mike Corbi, a forty-three-year-old Philadelphia-based agent for about twenty NFL players, sent a letter to Pete Rozelle that threatened legal action. In his March 26, 1986, letter, Corbi wrote:

> In the past several months, the topics of drug, steroid, and stimulant use in pro football has become a much discussed topic between my clients and myself. These discussions are prompted not by their concern about being tested themselves, but rather their concern of playing against players who are, as the players put it, "wired." My clients feel they cannot compete against such a player without exposing themselves to potential injury.
>
> If a program is not instituted, one that gives all the players in your league the protection against those who use controlled substances as a substitute for ability and conditioning, I will take legal action against the owners of the team, the Players Association, and the individual who is responsible, should one of my clients sustain a career-ending injury.

Dr. Daniel Begel, a psychiatrist, describes some of the problems connected with random testing.[9] For one thing, he says, urine testing does not separate out the occasional drug user from the addict. Dr. Begel feels that the athlete who gets "high" only occasionally is a user, not an abuser, of drugs. An abuser of drugs, according to Dr. Begel, is someone who uses substances for at least one month with the result that the person cannot function effectively without drugs. The test results, Begel argues, unfairly treats user and abuser the same way.

In Dr. Begel's view, the drug-testing plan proposed by Baseball Commissioner Ueberroth places all its emphasis on drug testing and getting rid of drug users. It shows almost no concern for helping players who are doing drugs. Also, Dr.

Begel feels that any attempt to rehabilitate drug users is doomed to failure if the drug-testing program is handled like a criminal procedure. Making drug testing central to the total drug prevention effort, Dr. Begel insists, actually glorifies drugs and interferes with other drug-abuse prevention activities.

Many therapists, including Dr. Begel, believe that the effectiveness of the testing program is weakened or destroyed if the results are made known to a third party. For drug testing to help the drug user, the findings must be kept confidential. Otherwise, the individual loses trust in the process.

The best way to combat drug abuse in sports, Dr. Begel claims, is to do something about the reasons that players turn to illegal substances in the first place. Among the athletes' problems are physical pain, job insecurity, great pressure to perform, extreme emotional highs and lows, encouragement to do drugs by the sports culture, and the constant presence of "thrill-seekers" who hang around the stars.

Robert Reid, thirty-one-year-old captain of the Houston Rockets, said that it is not unusual for him and his teammates to be offered drugs by strangers on a regular basis. "Out of a week, I'd say, I was approached six to eight times," he related. "I'll be in a restaurant or club and people will come up and say, 'Hey, I've got some blow in the trunk. Come on' . . . I got approached by a guy right outside the arena and got so mad that I slammed him against the wall and said, 'Listen, I don't do that, and you pass the word.' "

A number of professional ballplayers insist that management cares more for profits than for the athletes' well-being. Some owners even admit that they do not always look out for the players' best interests when it comes to drugs. "I don't think management has always treated employees properly," says Ballard Smith, president of the San Diego Padres.

In the past, treatment of players who tested positive has not always been fair. Lesser players with a suspected drug problem have often been traded to other clubs or sent to the minor leagues. In the case of star players, clubs tend either to ignore the test results or to rush the athlete through a quick drug-rehabilitation program and then back to the team. Dr. Joseph Pursch, who has treated many athletes for drug abuse, says that "once a guy gets back to the team, they don't want to hear about the problem." They say, "We are in the sports business, not the rehabilitation business."

DRUG TESTING AT THE RACETRACK

Early in 1985, the New Jersey State Racing Commission issued a regulation calling for breathalyzer and urine tests for all jockeys, as well as track officials, trainers, and grooms. The commission believes that the tests are necessary to protect the safety of jockeys on the track. The breathalyzer test is given to each jockey before each race to detect the presence of alcohol. At the end of the last race, the names of all jockeys who rode that day are placed in a large envelope, and three names are drawn. These three jockeys must then submit urine samples to be tested for the presence of illegal drugs.

On April 16, 1985, Willie Shoemaker, Angel Cordero, and three other well-known jockeys filed suit against the commission. They claimed that the regulation violated their right to privacy, in particular the Fourth Amendment protection against unreasonable search. They called the breathalyzer test "embarrassing" and the urine test "humiliating and degrading."

The jockeys also pointed out that this was the first time, outside of prisons, that "state officials were entitled to conduct warrantless searches of an individual's bodily fluids on a random basis, without so much as a reasonable suspicion that any of the individuals being searched had violated any law or rule."

A three-judge federal appeals court upheld a ruling by a New Jersey federal district court that the tests do not represent an invasion of privacy. According to the opinion, the public's need to trust the highly regulated horse-racing business outweighs any constitutional rights of the jockeys. The court said, "Frequent alcohol and drug testing is an effective means of demonstrating that persons engaged in the horse racing industry are not subject to outside influences."

On December 1, 1986, the Supreme Court refused to hear a challenge by the jockeys to the requirement that they submit to random testing. The Supreme Court's action was a big setback for the jockeys. But some experts insist that this ruling does not necessarily uphold mandatory drug testing. They believe that that question ultimately will be heard and settled by the highest court in the land.

6

TESTING IN
THE MILITARY

"Listen up, soldiers. When your life depends on the catlike reflexes and bullmoose strength of your buddies, you don't want
them strung out on drugs. If they're thinking they can get around
the Army's drug-testing program, they're wrong." So writes Gerri
Taylor in *Soldier,* an army magazine.

Because officials believe that drug-free personnel are vital
to national security, the military now gives about 3 million drug
tests a year to its 2.14 million soldiers, sailors, and marines.
These tests are currently designed to detect six types of drugs:
cocaine, marijuana, amphetamines, barbiturates, opiates, and
PCP.

The armed services conduct about one out of every two
drug tests in the nation.[10] According to Department of Defense
figures, the military drug program costs over $47 million a year.
It is the first but also the most thorough and ambitious drug-
testing program in the country.

Since the blanket testing began in 1981, drug taking appears to have declined dramatically in the military services.
Advocates say that these results prove that testing leads peo-

ple to stop using drugs. Opponents say that the results are misleading.

BACKGROUND

Urine testing first became part of soldiers' lives during the Vietnam War. Military personnel were performing many tasks requiring great care and accuracy. Some experts claimed that high levels of drug use were causing serious mistakes and leading to many instances of poor judgment. And since even a small error might cost lives, the Department of Defense set up a limited system of urine testing.

For several years after the Vietnam War, interest in drug testing waned. Then in December 1976, a study of sailors on the aircraft carrier U.S.S. Midway showed that a full 20 percent were using opiates and other drugs. At about the same time the heroin-overdose death rate for U.S. army soldiers in Europe jumped 50 percent above the previous year, making it three times as high as the civilian heroin-overdose death rate. In a survey conducted by the navy, 33 percent of all seamen admitted to using illegal drugs—mostly marijuana—within the previous month.

Some members of Congress were very distressed by these findings. They decided to hold hearings to determine if the security of the United States was being threatened by the high level of drug abuse in the military. After their deliberations they concluded that drugs were indeed a serious problem in the armed forces. Drug use had to be "contained" and "controlled."

Early in 1980 the Department of Defense did a study of the impact of drug and alcohol abuse on American military personnel. A total of 15,268 randomly selected men and women, stationed at eighty-one military bases around the world, filled out questionnaires anonymously. The answers indicated the extent of drug use among all military personnel.

Alcohol and marijuana showed up as the most abused drugs among enlisted members of the armed services. Of those using

these drugs, 31 percent reported some effect on their work performance due to alcohol use, and 21 percent said they suffered job impairment because of other drugs.

The data, however, did not support the widely held belief that the armed forces have a larger number of drug abusers than the general population. This mistaken idea was largely a carryover from the time of the Vietnam War. Nevertheless, the Department of Defense set out to curb the use of illicit drugs and alcohol in the military.

To combat the abuse of alcohol and the dangers of drunk driving, the Department of Defense instituted two measures. First, it decided to give a breathalyzer test for alcohol following any accident in which someone was injured. Second, it established maximum levels of alcohol in the blood to define impairment for duty, and third, it offered treatment and rehabilitation to any serviceman or servicewoman with a serious drinking problem.

The Armed Forces Institute of Pathology developed a special procedure for testing urine samples for marijuana in 1981. Testing for marijuana became the main goal of the defense department drug-abuse identification program. Members of the armed forces did not have the right to refuse testing, but they could contest the results.

Another survey was conducted in 1982. Again, the results showed that alcohol and marijuana were the most widely abused drugs by military personnel.[11] But the figures revealed a sharp decline in marijuana use.

Thus far, random drug testing has survived all challenges in the military courts. Two important decisions permitting the tests were made in *Murray v. Haldeman* in 1983 and *Commit-*

In 1971, a U.S. sergeant and "Fritz,"
one of five specially trained
dogs in Vietnam, check American
soldiers' baggage for marijuana.

tee for GI Rights v. Callaway in 1975. These cases emphasized the following points: When people join the military they accept the fact that they will have less privacy than civilians and that they will not be accorded the same protection under the Fourth Amendment as other citizens. And, the tests are considered necessary and justified because of the high incidence of drug abuse in the armed forces.

METHODS OF TESTING

Before entering military service, recruits are asked to sign a contract. The contract states that they will not use drugs and will not object to participating in the testing program.

Each branch of the military sets its own policy for deciding who is to be tested. Within that policy, each commander has wide discretion about how the tests are to be administered. Troops may be tested en masse or on an individual basis. Also, the commander can decide what to do with individuals who test positive.

The defense department laboratories first run a screening test on urine samples that have been collected. If no drug traces are present or if the amount of drug discovered is below the cutoff level, the finding is considered negative. If the test finds an amount above the cutoff level, the result is called positive.

The positive urine sample is then put through a more precise confirmation test. The army insists on two positive tests of the sample before declaring that an illicit drug is present. One negative test result, however, is all that is necessary to have a soldier declared officially "clean."

Once the tests are completed and the results are verified, the testing officials notify the unit commanders. The commanders then select a suitable option for those who come up positive on the urine test. The outcomes extend from enrollment in a drug-rehabilitation program to such disciplinary measures as confinement to quarters for several days, a diet of bread and

An army psychiatrist conducts a group
therapy session with drug-addicted servicemen.

water for seventy-two hours, loss of pay, or a dishonorable discharge.

According to Col. John Jewell, head of the drug-testing laboratory at Fort Meade, Maryland, commanders usually refer individuals to a local drug and alcohol center for counseling. "If no improvement has been made after the counseling, and further testing results indicate continued drug abuse, then discharge procedures are started," he says. This is in line with the army's basic philosophy that drug abuse has no place in military service.

The air force has recently begun requiring drug tests following accidents or mishaps. Testing is now automatically required for all crew members and ground personnel involved in serious airplane accidents. It is up to the commander to decide whether to test in less serious mishaps.

SOME DIFFICULTIES

The military set up its massive testing program in a remarkably short time. Perhaps that is why its first years were plagued with troubles. The laboratory results were attacked for being inaccurate, poorly managed, and unfair to innocent service people.

The problems started in 1982, at the very beginning of the navy's drug-testing program.[12] Four naval laboratories were performing up to 10,000 tests per month. Samples got mixed up. Jars were mislabeled. Tests were bungled by technicians who failed to clean containers adequately, leaving traces from one sample to contaminate others.

By July 1982, naval commanders began to question the large number of positive results. New tests were run on 6,000 positive tests reported between January and September 1982. Of these, 2,000 were "scientifically substantiated as positive," according to navy sources. Another 2,000 samples, though, were missing some form of identification. Error rates in labs used by the navy were in some instances found to be as high as 97 percent!

On the basis of these early tests, many thousands of sailors were discharged for drug abuse, even though a good number insisted that they had never taken drugs. Eventually, after recognizing the difficulties with the tests, 4,000 of the discharged sailors were reinstated. But considerable damage had already been done.

At first the army used the navy labs for its drug testing. But the army stopped this practice in 1982, after the many problems came to light.

As it turned out, many difficulties existed at the army's Fort Meade laboratory, as well. Chiefly, the army had trouble keeping track of the samples as they moved between the military bases and the testing laboratories.

Altogether, as reported in the July 27, 1984, issue of *American Medical News,* the army mishandled 52,000 urine samples tested for marijuana (60,000, according to other sources). Yet despite problems with testing techniques during 1982 and 1983, 34,000 members of the service were disciplined and 8,000 were discharged as a result of positive marijuana test results.

These unfortunate events led to the appointment of an investigative commission. In its March 1984 report, the commission stated that many of the problems had been solved. Also, it said that most of the errors were not related to the tests themselves. Rather, the mistakes had been due to poor management, inadequate personnel, a broken chain of custody, and faulty transfer of reports and records.

THE SITUATION TODAY

The Syva Company, which had the original contract to test military personnel with its EMIT urinalysis kits, blamed the inaccuracies on poor laboratory work, not the test itself. Nevertheless, in 1985 the army switched over to Abuscreen and also began a new testing program using gas chromatography/mass spectrometry (GC/MS).

The GC/MS test could detect marijuana traces in urine down to a level of 10 nanograms per milliliter. A nanogram is a billionth of a gram—an amount that weighs less than the eye of a fly. The greater sensitivity, the army felt, was needed since an average marijuana cigarette contains less than 3/1,000 of a gram of the active ingredient. Currently, the test is set up to detect levels as low as 20 nanograms per milliliter. "We can find this amount in the sample of someone who smoked a single joint as long as a week prior," says Colonel Jewell. "For a person who smokes on a regular basis, we can detect it up to three weeks later." But, he adds, "We are bending over backward to try to make sure no one is falsely accused."

Under the old test, Colonel Jewell notes, some soldiers got the idea that there were things they could do to hide drug abuse. "Drinking vinegar, adding soap or salt to the urine will not affect any of the testing," according to Colonel Jewell.

But a number of soldiers have expressed concern about the new marijuana test. What happens if they attend a rock concert and people around them are smoking pot? They breathe the marijuana smoke, and it enters their system. "Studies show that a person inhaling that smoke will show a low level," said Frank Gilliam, who heads the army's drug and alcohol testing laboratory in Falls Church, Virginia. "However, those studies also indicate that he's well below the level we test for." Those soldiers will not be judged as marijuana positive.

The purpose of drug testing in the military is, of course, to eliminate drug abuse. The latest survey indicates that drug abuse in the armed forces fell from 27 percent in 1980 to 9 percent in the fall of 1985.[13] In the navy alone, the number of seamen under age twenty-six who admitted the use of illegal drugs dropped from 47 percent to 4 percent in the same period.

The drug-testing company, Syva, claims that the apparent drop in positives among navy personnel, from 30 percent to 5 percent over the last several years, does not indicate a real drop in drug use (Newsweek, July 10, 1986). The decline, it says, was really due to raised minimum levels put into effect by the navy.

Kevin B. Zeese, executive director of the National Organization for the Reform of Marijuana Laws (NORML), questions the statistics in another way. He says that testing has not cut the use of all drugs. For example, The Army Times has reported that the percentage of servicemen and servicewomen using marijuana dropped from 38 to 25 percent in the first two years of testing. Meanwhile, though, the percentage of soldiers who reported that they were abusing alcohol and that it had decreased their performance shot up from 27 to 34 percent! Perhaps soldiers have merely substituted a legal drug (alcohol) for an illegal one (marijuana).

The testing of millions of samples is, at best, a difficult business. Tests that work well in small operations may not work as well in huge labs. Some problems may be due to the imperfect technology. Others may have to do with the imperfect nature of the humans who operate the machines. Surely the tedium of handling a never-ending flow of urine samples, hour after hour, day after day, has something to do with the mistakes that inevitably creep in.

SPACE AND DEFENSE

Recently there have been many calls to extend the military's drug-testing program to the space and defense industries. Although these industries are not part of the armed forces, they are very important to the military. Instances of accidents and negligence due to drugs in both the space program and the defense industry have led to a demand for drug testing in these areas.

Dr. Howard Frankel, medical director of Rockwell's space shuttle division from 1981 until 1983, says that during that time he treated employees who were hallucinating, collapsing from cocaine overdoses, and using marijuana, PCP, heroin, and numerous other drugs while at work. According to his estimates, 20 to 25 percent of the Rockwell workers at the Palmdale, California, plant, the final assembly point for the space shuttles, were high on the job from drugs, alcohol, or both. During the construction of the spacecraft, undercover agents were able to buy cocaine, heroin, amphetamines, and marijuana from employees. This led to a police raid on

Rockwell's shuttle assembly plant. As a result, nine workers were fired.

Obviously, any drug abuse among production workers in the space program or the defense industry carries grave risks. Says Dr. Frankel, "In this kind of ultra-high-tech work, the guy who makes the little adjustments, the screwer-on of parts, the bolter of nuts, is just as important as the project's chief engineer."

Besides fearing that "stoned" employees may do shoddy work on missiles and planes, defense industry executives are also concerned about security. Addicts on the payroll might sell defense secrets to support their habits. Or narcotics-possession charges could lead to the loss of the security clearances necessary for many jobs in the defense industry; this could make the drug abusers extremely vulnerable to blackmail. Says R. Richard Heppe, president of Lockheed California, "We do a lot of highly classified work here, and people with these problems are much higher security risks."

For these reasons, many experts have argued for extending the military's drug-testing program to the space and defense industries. But doing massive drug testing in privately owned businesses and in nonmilitary agencies of the government raises a special set of legal and ethical questions. The outcome remains uncertain.

7

TESTING IN
PRIVATE INDUSTRY

If you apply for a job at DuPont, the giant chemical company, the company will ask you for a urine specimen to be analyzed for the presence of illegal drugs. The company may insist that someone watch you give the sample to make sure that it is indeed your own. If the results come back positive, you will not be offered the job, no matter how well qualified you are.

If you apply for a job at Greyhound, the nationwide bus line, the procedure will be the same. The tests will determine whether you have recently used such drugs as heroin, cocaine, or amphetamines. They can even tell whether you have smoked marijuana within the past week or two.

You will also have to provide a urine sample and pass a drug test if you want a job with Westinghouse, Federal Express, Lockheed, Exxon, *The New York Times,* 3M, Southern Pacific, IBM, General Motors, TWA, Conrail, and hundreds of other companies big and small. The requirement is identical whether you have a history of drug use or have never been near an illegal substance. And it does not matter if you are applying for a job to work on a nuclear reactor or to sit at a typewriter. The result is the same: If you test positive for drugs, you won't get the job.

THE CURRENT SITUATION

Increasing numbers of American employers are now requiring drug tests for job applicants. And the number of companies who insist on tests for current employees is growing as well. Some of the companies require their workers to be tested when a supervisor thinks a person is doing poorly on the job, is exhibiting unusual behavior, or was involved in a recent accident. Others just give the test on a random basis, without any reason to suspect that the worker is impaired by drugs. If someone tests positive, the employer usually insists that the worker enter a drug-treatment program. If he or she refuses, the boss may fire the employee.

Dr. Douglas Lewis, head of a Chicago drug-testing laboratory, says that "roughly two-thirds of the drug tests given by industry are initial screenings only, without confirming tests." That means that positive indications of drugs are not double-checked. Even though the results say "tested positive," they might be false positives.

Out of every twenty people in a workplace tested for drugs, the chances are that one will get a false positive result.[14] The result may be dismissal or a blemish on that person's employment record for using drugs.

Laboratories that do industrial drug screening claim an error rate of less than one percent. But critics say that the error rates are much higher. An article in the *Journal of the American Medical Association* in April 1985 says that there is a "crisis in drug testing." Known samples submitted to thirteen drug laboratories showed error rates as high as 100 percent for certain drugs. "The results reflect serious shortcomings in the laboratories," the authors write.

No one knows exactly how many employers compel workers to pass drug tests. But according to the National Institute on Drug Abuse, 30 percent of the Fortune 500 companies—nearly one-third of the nation's largest private employers—have testing programs of some kind.[15] The majority of these companies

"There's nothing like pulling a surprise
drug test to keep the staff on their toes...!"

will not hire individuals who test positive for drugs. In 1985 alone, nearly 5 million Americans were tested for drugs—double the number of just two years ago!

The corporations feel fully justified in giving tests. For one thing, employers have a right to expect workers not to be high on the job, they say. Many argue that they have little choice but to test for drugs; in case of an accident caused by someone on drugs, employers without drug-testing programs might be considered at fault and have to bear the responsibility.

Imagine a situation, suggests Edward M. Bomsey of the Edison Electric Institute, in which an employee drives a company vehicle while under the influence of drugs. The employee gets high, then goes through a light and kills pedestrians. "Then I wonder," Bomsey says, "if those same critics would not ask why we weren't testing those guys every hour."

In response to critics of testing who say that testing is bad for company morale, some employers argue that testing actually improves morale. Robert W. Taggart of Southern Pacific, a company that does random testing of workers, said that of the hundreds of employees who have been required to take drug tests in his firm, only one has ever filed suit against the company.

It is a matter of record, though, that many workers oppose the tests. They claim that the tests violate their constitutional right to privacy. Some of them have gone on to challenge the various drug-testing programs in court.

Court cases of all kinds are now pending between workers and their employers. These cases raise two important issues: Can employers subject employees to body searches, even though there has been no suspicion of drug use? Do bosses have the right to monitor their workers' conduct off the job?

Despite the risk of lawsuits, the idea of making drug tests a condition of employment continues to spread. So far there have been few legal decisions that would convince private employers to stop testing. There are almost no legal limits on what private employers may do.

SCREENING
JOB APPLICANTS

Job seekers are tested for drugs more often than current employees. And there is no one that the applicant can turn to for help. As long as the tests are required of everyone, an applicant cannot claim discrimination.

If you apply for work in private industry, the employer can turn you away for almost any reason. You are protected against discrimination only on the basis of sex, race, or age.

In general, companies tend to be far more careless about testing job applicants than people already with the company. That is because employed workers tend to have more protection from their unions or other organizations.

In addition, some opponents point out that the screening tests are often done surreptitiously. A urine sample may be taken from a job applicant as part of a general physical examination, for example. The person who is not informed, of course, has no opportunity to contest the result.

Sloppy or inaccurate drug tests may give results that jeopardize someone's chances for employment, especially if no medical history has been taken. If you have a cold and take Contac, Sudafed, or any of several other perfectly legal cold medications, the test may indicate that you are using amphetamines. If you take certain cough syrups, the test may show traces of opiates. If you take an over-the-counter pain reliever, the test may show that you have been smoking marijuana. Since many companies do not bother to perform confirmations for job applicants whose tests are positive for drug use, the lack of retest can cost an applicant the job.

Although failing to perform backup tests on job applicants may be unfair, it is not illegal, according to Thomas E. Geidt, an attorney representing employers in San Francisco. "We don't feel that an employer is legally bound to do backup testing in a pre-employment situation."

Some drug-free people have gone to court claiming that they were denied jobs because the drug tests they were forced to take gave false positive results. They said that the test findings were incorrect and that they were being unjustly accused of doing drugs. Rulings have varied, depending on the particular circumstances, but usually the judges have favored the employers.

As more companies require job applicants to prove that they are drug free, it will probably become increasingly difficult to both use drugs and earn a living. Dr. J. Michael Walsh of the National Institute on Drug Abuse explains: "We feel that if Big Business continues as it has in the last year to develop more and more stringent kinds of policies, it eventually will reduce the demand for illicit substances. It may be very effective in changing the way people view drug taking in this country."

INVASION OF PRIVACY

Leslie Price and Susan Register are former employees of the Georgia Power Company. In 1984 they were working on a nuclear power plant construction project when the company began a drug-testing program. Workers were chosen at random and given urine tests. Also, a special hotline was set up for workers to report fellow employees whom they suspected of using drugs.

In early 1985 Price and Register were told they'd been "hotlined" and were ordered in for tests. The anonymous tip came soon after the two workers had reported company violations to the Nuclear Regulatory Commission. Register was asked to take a urine test in front of a nurse. Too humiliated to do so, she was fired for insubordination. Price was told that her sample was positive for marijuana and that she was being fired for misconduct.

In 1986, The New York Times and CBS News conducted a national poll on the American people's response to the drug-abuse problem. Seventy-two percent of the people polled answered "yes" to the question: "If your employer wanted to test all employees to determine if they had used illegal drugs recently, would you be willing to be tested, or would that be an unfair invasion of your privacy?" The large affirmative response

*"Along with your reports does everyone
have their urine sample?"*

was said to show that almost three-fourths of the American
people were willing to undergo urine testing for drugs in the
workplace.

Lloyd D. Johnston, the director of national surveys on drug
use at the University of Michigan, challenged the survey results. The question really has two parts, he wrote. The first is:
How would you feel about your employer giving drug tests to
workers to see if they are using drugs? The second is: Would
you comply if your employer required such urine tests? Johnston
believes that many who said "yes" might consider urine testing
an invasion of their rights. But, when faced with the choice, they
would comply rather than lose their jobs.

Not all employees who refuse employers' drug tests are
fired, but many are. For that reason, some workers feel victim-
ized by drug tests and raise objections to them. They dislike

having their cases handled in confidential hearings, rather than in open court. The overall effect can be intimidating. Some believe that the threat of testing can keep workers quiet—even to the point of endangering public safety.

One particularly significant lawsuit was filed in San Francisco in the summer of 1985. The case, *Luck v. Southern Pacific Transportation,* involved Barbara Luck, a computer programmer for the Southern Pacific Railroad in San Francisco. She had worked for the company for six years. One July morning Luck's supervisor, carrying a glass bottle, came over and asked her to go to the ladies' room and give a urine sample as part of the company's drug-testing program. Luck refused. The next day she was fired, even though the company admitted that she was an exemplary employee and had not been suspected of abusing drugs or alcohol.

Luck sued the railroad for invasion of privacy. She claimed that unless the company had reason to suspect her or found problems with her work, it had no right to test her. The case did not challenge Southern Pacific's right to test employees; it only tried to set limits on what an employer can do and under what conditions. According to Luck, her manager refused to believe that any employee would object to such a test on principle and took the position that she must be hiding something.

Testing is "a minor intrusion . . . like going through a metal detector at the airport," says Robert Taggart of Southern Pacific. Moreover, the company's counsel insists that the testing program represents a legitimate business interest. "Since testing began," Southern Pacific reports, "we have reduced our accident rate by 67 percent, and we have reduced lost time and injuries by over 25 percent." And they say that testing is consistent with a public policy that prohibits the use of illegal drugs and encourages rehabilitation.

Luck's lawyer acknowledged that Southern Pacific may have a legitimate reason to test some of its workers, particularly railroad workers, whose jobs may affect public safety. But as she pointed out, Luck's job was not in that category. Southern Pacific's business interest in drug testing, she argued, was not reason enough to invade Luck's privacy.

Dr. Harold M. Bates is a chemist with Metpath Laboratories of Teterboro, New Jersey, which performs drug tests. He suggests that urinalysis is an invasion of privacy for another reason. "A simple thing like urine can tell you a lot," he says. It can tell company officials whether an employee is being treated for a heart condition, manic-depressive illness, epilepsy, diabetes, or schizophrenia. The company might be tempted to get rid of workers with medical problems, he says, "even though they may be doing a perfectly good job." Several years ago, Dr. Bates recalls, a company fired an employee after learning from a urine test that he suffered from asthma. As it happened, in the Southern Pacific case, Barbara Luck did not want her employer to know that she was pregnant.

LIMITS TO TESTING

Many legal experts say that drug tests represent an unconstitutional attempt to control employees' behavior off the job. "An employer clearly has the right to determine whether someone is impaired on the job," says George Washington, a Detroit lawyer who has defended clients who were not hired, or were fired, because of positive urinalysis tests. "But if a company has the right to fire someone because they smoked marijuana on Saturday night, then they might start regulating whether people can get divorces, what their sleeping habits are, or whether they drink off duty."

The ACLU's Ira Glasser echoes this belief: "The employer has a legitimate interest in performance on the job, but not to delve into what people do off the job."

But many companies defend their right to do just that. Says Robert Taggart of Southern Pacific, "No one has a right to a job. We make one of the conditions of having a job here that a person be clean of drugs. When you come to work with drops of marijuana used on the weekend in your system, statistically I know that you will cost me more in productivity, in health-care costs, and in absenteeism."

Peter Bensinger, former head of the Drug Enforcement Administration, holds a view similar to Taggart's. "If somebody smokes pot on a Saturday night, it's the employer's business on Monday."

Those who are concerned about the legality of random drug testing agree that drug and alcohol abuse are costly and unsafe. But they insist that many employers' testing programs go beyond the requirements of protecting the health and safety of the workers or of good management. These critics say that the advocates of testing are trying to impose their own standards of behavior on those in their employ. Employers respond that unauthorized use of controlled substances is against the law, not just aberrant behavior.

Some labor unions straddle the fence on the drug-testing issue. On the one hand, they want employers to assure a safe, drug-free workplace to protect their members from being involved in accidents or costly mistakes. But at the same time, they also share the concern of civil libertarians for the constitutionally guaranteed right to privacy.

As one union leader sees it, the "rage of testing may exacerbate the drug problem." By that he means that corporate crackdowns may make employees less willing to come forward and seek treatment. If companies want to eliminate drug abuse, he says, they should make treatment programs available to employees with problems, instead of just testing them for drugs.

Some unions that oppose testing do not wish to look as if they are in favor of drug use either. In March 1986, the International Brotherhood of Teamsters negotiated a mutually acceptable drug-testing contract with the trucking industry. The contract balances the protection of employee privacy with a concern for public safety and company productivity. It sets limits on when testing may take place and requires that treatment be made available for those who test positive. Former substance users who become drug free and remain "clean" can retain their jobs.

"A HARASSMENT TOOL"

Union leaders also worry about the possibility of drug tests being used for unscrupulous purposes. One union president has been tested five times in three months, according to James Moran, director of the union-sponsored Philadelphia Area Project on Occupational Safety and Health. The company "is using it as a harassment tool," he says.

In another incident involving Southern Pacific, thirty-year-old office manager Alan Pettigrew agreed to submit to a urine test. He tested positive for cocaine. Pettigrew denied that he used any drug except a nonprescription allergy medicine. He was told he could take another test but that, regardless of results, he would have to undergo a five-day hospital evaluation program before being allowed to return to work. The result of the second test was negative.

Southern Pacific, nonetheless, forced Pettigrew to attend a twenty-eight-day in-hospital rehabilitation program and to participate either in Alcoholics Anonymous or in Narcotics Anonymous. Says his lawyer, Richard N. Dinallo, "They gave him nine or ten follow-up tests, and they all were negative. Even the doctors at the clinic say there was no need for rehabilitation." Despite these continuing negative tests, Pettigrew was required to fulfill all the conditions that had been set and to submit to regular testing.

Eventually, in November 1985, Pettigrew filed suit to put an end to the testing. He charged the company with invasion of privacy and false imprisonment following a false positive drug test (*Pettigrew v. Southern Pacific Transportation Company*).

In December a Superior Court judge issued an injunction to stop Southern Pacific from further testing, pending resolution of the case. The day after the injunction came down, Pettigrew was demoted to a nonmanagement job at decreased pay and benefits.

Alfred Klein, a Los Angeles attorney, has experience in settling disputes between employers and workers. He points out another drawback in relation to employee drug testing. Excellent workers who test positive sometimes admit to casual use of a substance when questioned, but out of embarrassment, they feel obliged to leave the firm. Often, he says, their leaving is against the firm's wishes and best interests and can mean a real loss for the company.

PROTECTING THE RIGHTS
OF EMPLOYEES

A huge uproar followed the Barbara Luck–Southern Pacific case. As a result, the city of San Francisco passed the first law limiting drug testing in the private sector. In November 1985 the city barred all employers doing business in the city from ordering blood or urine tests. The only exception is when there is clear evidence that a worker's drug use endangers others. The law permits tests only for such emergency service workers as police, fire fighters, and rescue units.

Legislation to restrict or regulate drug testing has been or is now being considered by the states of Oregon, Maryland, and California. Maine Senator Charles P. Pray introduced a bill similar to San Francisco's ordinance in Congress during the spring of 1986.

In Maryland, legislators tried to pass the nation's first law limiting an employer's ability to use urinalysis and other tests to detect mind-altering drugs in their workers' bodies. This "model" bill would have required companies to prove that the tests they use show impairment or intoxication on the job. But it would not have prevented employers from requiring drug tests. It would have prohibited them from taking disciplinary action, including the firing of workers, on the basis of test results obtained in wholesale drug-testing programs. The bill died in committee in mid-1986, however.

"We're not against the employer's right to test his employees," said Maryland delegate Nathaniel Exum. "We just want to make sure they don't use the test to make wrong decisions about the worker."

The Maryland legislation would have left a door open for urine testing. But it would have used the urine test as a way to find and help drug users, through counseling and rehabilitation, rather than punish them.

Those who argued against this proposal said it would send mixed signals to Maryland corporations and their employees. "It would protect illegal activity," said the head of one law firm. "It takes the heart and soul out of the drug test, which is the disciplinary action that would follow a positive test." He questioned Maryland's ability to attract major companies, many of which have drug-testing programs, should the state refuse to allow businesses to test employees.

The National Institute on Drug Abuse sponsored a major conference on testing in the workplace in 1986 to search out areas of agreement. The conference brought together civil libertarians, representatives of corporations, and scientists. It prepared a set of voluntary guidelines for drug testing that might provide a road map for corporate testing.

The group reached agreement on the following points:

1. All people tested must be informed that they are being tested.

2. An employee cannot be tested without a clear job-performance problem—either an accident or an obvious decline in effectiveness at work.

3. All positive tests must be confirmed through use of alternate tests.

4. Test results must remain confidential.

5. Use of urinalysis must be accompanied by drug rehabilitation.

While society still struggles to find a meeting of minds on the issue of drug testing, we can expect a stormy period of trial and error ahead. Some lawyers say it will take years before all the abuses and excesses of drug testing will be curbed by the courts and the local, state, and federal legislatures. Says Robert Taggart of Southern Pacific, "We're all groping in the dark because it's so new."

The words of a forty-year-old woman who was forced to take a urine test in the presence of her employer's washroom attendant summarizes the dilemma of testing in private industry. "I am," she said, "all for keeping drugs out of every place in America. But can't there be some respect and privacy brought into this awful situation?"

8

TESTING IN
THE PUBLIC SECTOR

On September 15, 1986, President Ronald Reagan issued an executive order requiring random drug testing of federal government civilian employees in so-called "sensitive" positions. The Office of Personnel Management estimates that over 1 million persons are involved.[16] Under the executive order, employees with confirmed positive test results could be disciplined or even dismissed from their jobs.

Proponents of drug testing say the plan is needed as part of an overall strategy to achieve a drug-free workplace. They say this despite the lack of evidence that there is extensive drug abuse among government workers.

By reducing the number of employees abusing drugs, the government hopes to cut the "lifeblood" of organized crime. As Judge Irving R. Kaufman, head of the President's Commission on Organized Crime, puts it, "Law enforcement has been tested to the utmost. But let's face it: it hasn't succeeded. So let's try something else. Let's try drug testing."

PRO AND CON

Even government officials are divided on the advisability of drug testing of federal employees. On the same day that President Reagan issued his order, Rep. Charles E. Schumer (Democrat, New York) introduced legislation into Congress placing limits on testing in government and industry. The following day, seventeen cosponsors submitted another bill to Congress restricting drug testing by federal agencies.

Here is a small sample of favorable reactions to the government's drug-testing plan:

- Urine testing is "a death blow to the drug culture. What you're seeing is that the American public is saying 'We're fed up, tired of drugs, and whatever it takes to do it, let's do it,' " says Dr. Carlton E. Turner, former director of the White House drug policy office.

- "There are no civil rights when it comes to taking drugs, none whatsoever," says Arthur Brill of the President's Commission on Organized Crime.

- "Drug testing is a means to provide a safer workplace," says Peter Bensinger, former head of the Drug Enforcement Administration.

And here are some reactions of disapproval:

- "Testing like that is repugnant in our system," says Rep. Don Edwards (Democrat, California), chair of the House Subcommittee on Civil and Constitutional Rights.

- "Wholesale testing is unwarranted and raises serious civil liberties concerns," says Rep. Peter Rodino (Democrat, New Jersey), chair of the House Judiciary Committee.

- "A war on drugs is a good idea, but not if its first casualty is the Bill of Rights," says Stephen Sachs, Maryland attorney general.

Law experts point out that, unlike workers in private industry, government employees may claim the protection of the

U.S. Constitution. The chief issue raised by court cases that challenge drug testing of federal employees is whether the programs violate the Fourth Amendment. For that reason, it is important to take a closer look at the amendment itself and how it came to be.

THE FOURTH AMENDMENT

The Fourth Amendment to the Constitution came directly out of the rough treatment suffered by colonists at the hands of Great Britain before the creation of the United States. To protect its empire, the Crown restricted trade between the colonies and imposed high import duties on goods entering the colonies from outside the empire.

As a result, smuggling became widespread and was practiced by even the most respectable colonists. In order to enforce their harsh laws, British soldiers frequently conducted unrestricted house-to-house searches. People were forced to keep their private records and other personal information on their person or hidden in their home or business to avoid exposure and possible arrest.

The Fourth Amendment was made part of the Constitution's Bill of Rights to protect people's privacy and set limits on the government's power to search people and their homes and businesses. It provides that the "right of the people to be secure in their persons, houses, papers, and effects, against unreasonable searches and seizures, shall not be violated."

Today, privacy rights have more to do with the basic quality of an individual's personal life—the rights to keep the details of that life confidential, to choose one's own lifestyle, to associate with whom one chooses—in sum, the right to a life free from government interference or the dictates of society.

The right to privacy was described by Supreme Court Justice Louis D. Brandeis as "the right to be let alone—the most comprehensive of rights and the right most valued by civilized men." No matter how compelling a government's need to pursue a given policy, the individual's right to privacy, many believe, must serve as a check. Many consider the Fourth Amendment the most effective barrier to the threat of a police state and the "Big Brother" mentality.

TROUBLE IN THE COURTS

In the months following President Reagan's drug-testing order, a number of court cases arose. All of them challenged the constitutionality of the random screening of government employees. The heart of the matter is whether tests requiring employees to provide urine samples for testing are legally equivalent to the search of homes or bodies. If they are, then drug testing goes against the Fourth Amendment.

Employees who defy the government's testing program argue that drug testing is a search and that they are being deprived of Fourth Amendment protection. Government lawyers defend random testing by insisting that a urine test is not at all the same as a search of a home or a body. They claim that it is more like the blood test everyone must take when applying for a marriage license or the routine fingerprinting of employees for security reasons. Just as neither of these two practices violates constitutional rights, urine tests should not be considered illegal.

Alan F. Westin, professor of public law at Columbia University, points out that the courts are striking down the government's testing program in case after case. As he says, "The courts are turning a hostile face to random testing of government employees."

A survey published in *The New York Times* on December 11, 1986, found at least thirteen cases in which a judge ruled that drug testing of government workers violates the Fourth Amendment protections against unreasonable searches and seizures. The testing program has been upheld in only four cases.

Professor Westin explains why he feels so many judges are handing down negative decisions. Generally, he says, it has to do with the loss of dignity and privacy involved in giving a urine sample, the error rate in the commonly used drug tests, and the fact that the tests only measure the amount of a drug in the person's system and not whether it affects his or her functioning on the job.

In 1986 alone, federal judges ruled against testing programs in Georgia, New Jersey, Tennessee, and Louisiana. The affected workers were police officers, fire fighters, and U.S. Customs Service agents. In issuing his verdict in the customs service employees' case, Judge Robert F. Collins of the federal district court in New Orleans wrote, "This dragnet approach, a large-scale program of searches and seizures made without probable cause or even reasonable suspicion, is repugnant to the Constitution."

The first case to question the right of a government agency to give screening tests to all job applicants was heard in late 1986. The suit claimed that drug tests given to all people seeking jobs with the Philadelphia Post Office violated the Fourth Amendment. Before the program was stopped, 230 prospective employees were turned away because of positive test results. The suit also charged that the tests could not distinguish between illegal drugs and prescription drugs taken for such conditions as epilepsy—a violation of the Federal Rehabilitation Act of 1973, which prohibits discrimination against the handicapped.

As a result of the ruling, the Post Office stopped giving drug tests to job applicants. It also paid a sum of $55,000 to eleven workers who had satisfied all the requirements for employment but were denied the job because of test evidence.

The negative trend of court decisions is making municipalities stop and rethink their proposals for employee screening. The Los Angeles Police Commission, for instance, had prepared a plan for the random testing of 7,000 police officers. On December 9, 1986, though, Assistant City Attorney Leslie E. Brown advised the commission that the courts would probably rule such testing illegal. Brown reported, "I don't think that they [the commission] will go ahead with the random testing. The decisions put a pretty big impediment before them."

Many think that government testing programs will be found unconstitutional unless the authorities have either reasonable suspicion or probable cause that the individuals being tested are on drugs. As Prof. Abraham S. Goldstein of the Yale Law School says, "It is fairly clear that the broad-scale generalized testing programs are just too broad."

REASONABLE SUSPICION

Very early on the morning of May 26, 1986, fire fighters at the firehouse in the city of Plainfield, New Jersey, were awakened at 7 A.M. and ordered to submit urine samples in a surprise drug test. The same procedure was followed on May 28 and June 12, so that samples were obtained from all 103 members of the fire department. At about the same time, employees of the Plainfield police department were subjected to similar unannounced urine testing.

Between July 10 and July 14, sixteen fire fighters and one member of the police department were advised that they had tested positive for illegal drugs. They were immediately discharged from their jobs. The discharged fire fighters, along with the police officer, decided to bring their case to court.

The issue before the court was simple. Given the government's interest in ferreting out drug abuse, was compulsory urine testing by the Plainfield Fire Department "reasonable" under the Fourth Amendment?

On September 18, 1986, Judge H. Lee Sarokin of the federal district court in Newark handed down his ruling. Mandatory urine testing of government employees, such as the fire fighters in Plainfield, violated the Fourth Amendment.

In this instance, the fire fighters had been forced to give urine samples without notice and in the presence of the other fire fighters. Those who tested positive were discharged without being given a chance to appeal. Only a reasonable suspicion that a certain individual was using illegal drugs could justify such an action, the court held. "In order to win the war against drugs, we must not sacrifice the life of the Constitution in the battle," said Judge Sarokin.

PROBABLE CAUSE

A number of public sector court cases hinge on the question of probable cause. Was there sufficient evidence of impairment and lowered performance on the job to warrant testing and dismissal?

The case of *Jones v. McKenzie* in 1986 brought about a significant decision. Involved here was a school bus attendant, Juanita Jones, who worked for the Washington, D.C., schools helping handicapped children on and off the buses. In a mandatory drug test, Jones tested positive, and the school board dismissed her. She said that the test violated the Fourth Amendment. The school admitted that it had no probable cause for suspicion. But it argued that the test and dismissal were reasonable because bus attendants on drugs threaten the safety of the children.

The court agreed with Jones. It ruled that the public school system could not administer a urine test for drug use to a school bus attendant without first establishing probable cause that the employee was under the influence of drugs.

Prison officials in Iowa recently received an anonymous tip that a particular guard was using drugs. When the guard was asked to submit a urine sample for testing, he refused and was suspended without pay. The guard took the case to court. In the 1985 case, *McDonell v. Hunter,* the state argued that it had to identify drug smugglers within the prisons and to keep its correctional staff drug free.

In his decision against the state, Judge Harold D. Vietor, chief judge of the federal district court in Des Moines, reinstated the prison guard in his job and awarded him back pay. He said that a government agency must show the same kind of probable cause to test an individual's urine as is needed to search a person's house or tap his or her telephone.

"There is no doubt about it," wrote Judge Vietor, "searches and seizures can yield a wealth of information to the searchers. (That is why King George III's men so frequently searched the colonists.) That potential, however, does not make a governmental employer's search of an employee a constitutionally reasonable one."

EXTRAORDINARY CIRCUMSTANCES

When public employees have challenged the right of government agencies to test for drugs, the courts have usually found in the employee's favor. Sometimes, though, an agency's right to test has been sustained. This is especially likely if the agency's employees are responsible for national security or public health and safety.

One of the earliest cases involving urine testing of government employees to reach the courts was *Division 241 Amalgamated Transit Union v. Suscy.* In 1976 the union, representing 5,500 bus drivers, challenged the constitutionality of the Chicago Transit Authority's drug-testing requirement. The Transit Authority demanded that bus operators who are suspected of using narcotics or alcohol or become involved in a serious accident submit to blood and urine tests.

After due deliberation, the court decided that the drug tests were reasonable, considering the Transit Authority's "paramount" interest in the public's safety. According to the court's decision, the concern for public safety had priority over the bus drivers' right to privacy under the Fourth Amendment.

In 1985 a federal district court in Atlanta ruled in *Allen v. City of Marietta* that city employees who worked on high-voltage electric wires could be forced to submit to urine tests. The tests were given after an undercover agent, who was planted among the workers, observed some of the employees smoking marijuana at work. Employees who were suspected of doing drugs on the job were told either to submit urine samples or to resign. The court ruled that the tests were reasonable in light of the extremely dangerous nature of the work and the careful nature of the investigation.

Several cases have upheld the testing of police and corrections officers, whether conducted at random or "for cause." In *Turner v. Fraternal Order of Police* in 1985, the federal circuit court for the District of Columbia upheld a police department rule allowing drug tests where there is suspicion of drug use. Police department regulations allowing drug testing of police force members do not violate the Fourth Amendment as long as officials have reason to believe that a urine test would yield evidence of illegal drug use.

"Given the nature of [police] work and the fact that not only his life, but the lives of the public rests upon [an officer's] alertness, the necessity of rational action and a clear head unbefuddled by narcotics becomes self evident," the court said. "The use of controlled substances by police officers creates a situation fraught with serious consequences to the public." Consequently, the current widespread drug use by all segments of the population justifies the department's action in requiring drug tests of the police officers.

In August 1986 the New York State Supreme Court rejected a challenge to the testing of corrections officers who drive prison vans and buses for New York City. The opinion cited the strong security and safety considerations involved in transporting prisoners.

WORKERS IN
REGULATED INDUSTRIES

Elizabeth Hanford Dole, Secretary of Transportation, supports drug testing of workers in the aviation, railroad, trucking, and bus industries, all of which are regulated by her department. In December 1986, Secretary Dole set out her reasons. She said, "Where the safe transportation of the public is concerned, there can be no tolerance for drug or alcohol abuse. We need to find the best ways to enforce rigorous standards concerning drug and alcohol abuse."

*Miami police officers voluntarily agreeing to
take urine tests to show they are not using drugs*

Dole made these comments just after the Federal Aviation Administration (FAA) announced a mandatory testing proposal for pilots and other airline personnel. The proposal begins, "Drug and alcohol abuse are a major problem in society." Then it says, "The FAA does not have any conclusive information that drug use and alcohol abuse among personnel engaged in aviation activities is any lesser or greater than that of the general public." But the agency is "concerned that abuse may exist based on the overall use of drugs among the general populace."

Officials of the FAA assert that no scheduled U.S. airliner has ever been involved in an accident caused by drug taking in which lives were lost. But Jim Burnett, head of the National Transportation Safety Board, notes that in 1983 and 1984 there were ten private aircraft accidents in which the pilots were suspected of having taken drugs.

The proposed rules would apply to private airplane pilots as well as to airline flight crews and aviation mechanics. The rules include: mandatory drug testing of all current employees on a random basis as well as on a regular schedule; drug-screening tests of all job applicants; absolutely no use of illegal drugs, even when off duty; special tests when there is a "reasonable suspicion" of drug use; and the provision of education, training, and rehabilitation services for employees.

The rules are being added to existing FAA regulations for airline and private airplane personnel. These regulations state that no one may serve in flight while using a drug "that adversely affects faculties necessary for safety." Anyone found guilty of such drug use, of possessing or selling drugs, or of refusing to be tested can have his or her license revoked or suspended for up to a year.

The concern for the safety of the traveling public also extends to the railroads and highways. Between 1975 and 1985 there were forty-eight drug- or alcohol-related accidents on U.S. railroads. They left thirty-seven people dead, eighty injured, and $34 million in damage. As a result, the Federal Railroad Administration (FRA) issued some special rules in 1985. The regulations included preemployment drug screens for applicants and tests for employees suspected by supervisors of impairment caused by drugs. In addition, the regulations required railroad employees involved in any accidents to be tested for drug and alcohol use immediately after the accident. The maximum penalty for using illegal drugs or alcohol on the job is $2,500 per violation.

Soon after the regulations were announced, the railway workers brought the matter to court. Judge Charles Legge of the federal district court in 1985 handed down an important ruling. He said that the need to guarantee public safety outweighed the employees' Fourth Amendment protection.

On Sunday, January 4, 1987, three Conrail locomotives were struck by a speeding Amtrak train. The accident, which killed 16 people and injured more than 170, was the worst disaster in Amtrak's history. Drug tests after the collision showed traces of marijuana in the blood and urine of the engineer and brakemen operating the Conrail engines. Intoxication with marijuana is known to slow down reactions and cause difficulty in making routine decisions.

Whether the men were intoxicated at the time of the accident, though, is open to some question. According to Dr. Norman Zinberg of the Harvard Medical School and Richard Weisman, director of New York's Poison Control Center, two experts who were asked for their opinion, intoxication would depend on when they had smoked the marijuana and how often they used the drug. In addition to possible drug use, W. Graham Claytor, Amtrak chairman, said at least six safety rules, including equipment tampering, may have been responsible for the accident.

Nevertheless, government officials immediately began questioning the effectiveness of the present alcohol and drug abuse rules. Many called for new mandatory random drug testing of transportation workers. Transportation Secretary Elizabeth Dole, for example, proposed random tests for thousands of employees including air traffic controllers and inspectors for airlines, the trucking industry, and railroads. "When it

The wreckage from the 1987 train accident
in which sixteen people were killed.
Tests showed that the engineer and brakemen
of the Conrail engines had been using marijuana.

comes to drug abuse in transportation, there can be no compromise," she said. Meanwhile, Lawrence Mann, a Washington lawyer who represents rail workers, expressed his strong opposition to random testing.

The Federal Highway Administration also restricts the use of drugs among some of its workers. It requires that interstate truck drivers and bus drivers not use amphetamines, narcotics, or any other habit-forming drugs. New legislation now being considered would make it a federal offense to operate a common carrier truck or bus while under the influence of drugs. Anyone found guilty of this crime could receive a prison sentence of not more than five years or a fine of not more than $10,000, or both.

SUMMARY

Not long ago Rodney Smith, deputy executive director of the President's Commission on Organized Crime, was waiting to testify before the Civil Service Subcommittee of the House of Representatives. He was going to speak out in favor of making urine tests mandatory for all federal workers. Before hearing his testimony, Chairman Gary Ackerman asked Smith to submit a sample of urine that would be checked for traces of marijuana, cocaine, amphetamines, and barbiturates.

"The chair will require you to go to the men's room under the direct observation of a male member of the subcommittee staff to urinate in this specimen bottle," Congressman Ackerman said as aides placed a three-inch plastic specimen bottle on the witness table. Startled, Smith angrily refused, saying he had not been warned that such a test would be necessary for him to testify.

Congressman Ackerman did not insist. He merely pointed out that Smith's protests underscored the subcommittee's concerns about the federal government's right to demand drug tests of its employees without reasonable suspicion or probable cause that such tests should be administered.

Some say that asking a federal employee to take a drug test is no more harmful than asking a person to read an eye chart when applying for a license to drive a car. "The reason we give an eye test is not only to protect the person taking the exam but the rest of society," said Arthur Brill, speaking for the President's Commission on Organized Crime. "That's exactly what we're saying regarding drug testing."

Those who criticize that rationale say it is silly to pretend you can put the bad guys out of business by testing a million or more federal workers for signs of drug abuse. Andrew Feinstein, chief counsel of the House Subcommittee on Civil Service, has said that the committee used a "most Rube Goldbergish route of logic," meaning that it was twisted and overly intricate, like the sculptures of Rube Goldberg.

In support of federal testing, it has been suggested that accepting public employment and knowing that there will be random testing is really implied consent to the testing, which eliminates any Fourth Amendment problems. Attorney General Edwin Meese III says drug testing is not an unreasonable search "because it's something an employee consents to as a condition of employment."

But in the court cases judges have ruled that consenting to random drug testing as a condition of government employment *does not* satisfy Fourth Amendment requirements. Forcing an individual to make a choice between giving up a constitutional right and losing a job applies unfair pressure.

Experts on constitutional law differ over the issue of drug testing for government employees. "This is the opening chapter in a story where the final chapter has not been written yet," said Dr. Henry P. Monaghan, professor of law at Columbia University. And he adds that eventually the U.S. Supreme Court will have to rule on this important question.

FOR FURTHER
INFORMATION

American Civil Liberties Union
132 West 43rd Street
New York, NY 10019

Editorial Resources, Inc.
P.O. Box 21133
Washington, DC 20009

National Clearinghouse for Drug Abuse Information
P.O. Box 416
Kensington, MD 20795

National Institute on Drug Abuse
5600 Fishers Lane
Rockville, MD 20850

Roche Diagnostics, Inc.
340 Kingland Street
Nutley, NJ 07110

Syva Company
900 Arastradero Road
Palo Alto, CA 94304

GLOSSARY

Abuscreen. The most widely used radioimmunoassay drug test.

Amphetamines. A group of drugs that stimulate the central nervous system and promote a feeling of alertness and an increase in speech and general physical activity.

Barbiturates. A group of sedatives that includes drugs with such trade names as Phenobarbital, Nembutal, and Seconal.

Chain of custody. A way of handling samples from the time they are taken from the individual, through the lab, and until the final results are received.

Cocaine. A drug extracted from the leaves of the coca plant that increases heart rate and blood pressure. Street cocaine is a powder that is most commonly inhaled. See also *Crack*.

Confirmation. A second drug test that uses a method other than the first to positively identify a drug.

Controlled drugs. A group of substances that are regulated by law based on their dangerous effects and potential for abuse.

Crack. A smokable form of cocaine that is the most toxic form of the drug.

Cross reactivity. A positive result in a drug screening for substances other than the drug being treated for.

Drug. Any chemical substance that produces physical, mental, emotional, or behavioral changes in the user.

Drug Abuse. The use of a drug for other than medicinal purposes, which results in harm to the physical, mental, emotional, or social well-being of the user.

Drug dependence. A need to continue taking a drug often despite adverse social and medical consequences.

Drug misuse. The unintentional or inappropriate use of prescription or over-the-counter drugs that results in harm to the user.

Drug test. A way to detect illegal drug use and deter it. Usually by urinalysis.

EIA. Short for *enzyme immunoassay.* A drug test that is based on an enzyme (protein) producing a chemical reaction that is directly related to the concentration of the drug present in the urine.

EMIT. Short for *enzyme multiplied immunoassay technique.* It is the most frequently used enzyme immunoassay test in the country.

False negative. An erroneous result that indicates the absence of a drug that is actually present in the sample.

False positive. An erroneous result that indicates the presence of a drug that is actually not present.

Flashback. A recurrence of some effects of a past LSD experience days or months after the last dose.

GC/MS. Short for *gas chromatography/mass spectrometer.* The most conclusive method of confirming the presence of a drug in urine.

Hallucinogens. A group of drugs that affect perception, sensation, thinking, self-awareness, and emotion.

Illicit drugs. Drugs whose use is forbidden by law.

LSD. Short for *lysergic acid diethylamide.* A synthetic hallucinogen that basically causes changes in the user's sensations. Vision, sense of time, and sense of self are altered.

Marijuana. A common plant that contains a psychoactive ingredient commonly called THC.

Mescaline. A natural hallucinogen from the peyote cactus.

Narcotics. A group of drugs that relieves pain and often induces sleep. It includes the opiates and certain synthetic chemicals such as methadone.

Opiates. A group of drugs that includes opium and drugs derived from opium, such as morphine, codeine, and heroin.

Paranoia. A mental disorder characterized by suspicion and thoughts of supposed hostility in others.

PCP. Short for *phencyclidine.* A drug that produces delirium, extreme excitement, and visual disturbances in users. Also called "angel dust."

Psychedelics. A group of drugs, including LSD and mescaline, that produce intensified sensory perceptions in users. Also called *hallucinogens.*

Psychoactive drugs. Drugs that have mind-altering properties.

Quaaludes. A trade name for methaqualone, a kind of sedative that has such possible effects as slurred speech and disorientation.

RIA. Short for *radioimmunoassay.* A drug test similar to EMIT.

Schizophrenia. A severe mental illness characterized by withdrawal, bizarre, and sometimes delusional behavior.

Sedatives. A group of drugs that depress the central nervous system. Also known as tranquilizers and sleeping pills.

Stimulants. A group of drugs that stimulate the central nervous system and produce an increase in alertness and activity.

TLC. Short for *thin-layer chromatography.* The most practical technique for large-scale screening for various drugs.

Tolerance. A need to take larger and larger doses of a drug to get the same effects.

Urinalysis. A chemical or microscopic examination of a urine sample for purposes of diagnosing a condition or identifying a substance in the urine.

Valium. A commonly prescribed sedative used to counter anxiety and promote relaxation.

Withdrawal symptoms. The uncomfortable experiences in users who stop taking a drug to which their bodies have become accustomed.

NOTES

CHAPTER 1

[1] Department of Health and Human Services, National Institute on Drug Abuse, Data, 1985.
[2] Joel Brinkley, "U.S. Says Cocaine-Related Deaths are Rising," *The New York Times,* 10 July 1986, sec. 1, p. 1.
[3] Sam Fulwood III, "Tests of Workers a Thorny Case for Company Lawyers," *Baltimore Sun,* 17 March 1986, sec. 1, p. 5.

CHAPTER 2

[4] Joel Brinkley, "Drug Use Held Mostly Stable or Lower," *The New York Times,* 9 October 1986, sec. 1, p. 14.

CHAPTER 3

[5] Richard Pollak, "A Bitter Pill for Epileptics," *The New York Times,* 3 September 1986, sec. 1, p. 26.
[6] Richard H. Schwartz and Richard L. Hawks, "Laboratory Detection of Marijuana," *Journal of the American Medical Association,* 9 August 1985, vol. 254, no. 6, p. 791.
[7] John Lang and Ronald Taylor, "America on Drugs," *U.S. News and World Report,* 28 July 1986.

CHAPTER 4
[8] Willard L. Hogeboom, "Proposals for Drug Testing," *The New York Times,* 30 November 1986.

CHAPTER 5
[9] Daniel Begel, M.D., "Medical Problems of Random Tests," *The New York Times,* 26 May 1985, sec. 5, p. 2.

CHAPTER 6
[10] Lawrence K. Altman, "Drug Tests Gain Precision But Can Be Inaccurate," *The New York Times,* 16 September 1986.
[11] "Alcohol and Drug Abuse Among American Military Personnel," *Alcohol, Health and Research World,* Winter 85/86, vol. 10, no. 2.
[12] John P. Morgan, M.D., "Problems of Mass Urine Screening for Misused Drugs," *Journal of Psychoactive Drugs,* October–December 1984, vol. 16.
[13] Robert Angarola, "Protect Safety, Not Drug Abuse," *American Bar Association Journal,* 1 August 1986, p. 35.

CHAPTER 7
[14] Robert G. Newman, M.D., "Pro and Con Drug Testing in the Workplace," *The New York Times,* 7 September 1986.
[15] Robert Willette, "Drug Testing Programs," *NIDA Research Monograph 73,* 1986, p. 10.

CHAPTER 8
[16] Lena Williams, "Reagan Drug Testing Plan," *The New York Times,* 28 November 1986, sec. 1, p. 1.

SOURCES

NEWSPAPERS
AND MAGAZINES:

The Baltimore Sun
"The Cup Runneth Over," August 22, 1986
"Test of Workers a Thorny Case for Company Lawyers," March 17, 1986

Harper's
"What is Our Drug Problem?" December 1985

Newsday
"Types of Tests and Reliability Vary," March 10, 1986
"Tougher Drug Tests Asked for Trainmen," January 21, 1987

Newsweek
"Trying to Say 'No'," August 11, 1986
"A Question of Privacy," September 29, 1986

The New York Times
"Pro & Con: Testing for Drugs in the Schools," November 10, 1985
"The Validity of Student Drug Testing," December 10, 1985
"Pro & Con: Drug Testing in the Workplace," September 7, 1986

"Drug Test," September 16, 1986
"The Battle Over Drug Testing," October 19, 1986
"Employee Privacy and Employers' Rights," October 19, 1986
"FAA May Require Testing," December 5, 1986
"Drug Tests Losing Most Court Cases," December 12, 1986
"U.S. Says Cocaine Related Deaths Are Rising," July 10, 1986
"Drug Use Held Mostly Stable or Lower," October 9, 1986
"A Bitter Pill for Epileptics," September 3, 1986
"Proposals for Drug Testing," November 30, 1986
"Medical Problems of Random Tests," May 26, 1985
"Drug Tests Gain Precision But Can Be Inaccurate," September 16, 1986
"Reagan Drug Testing Plan," November 28, 1986
"Right to Privacy is a Basic Principle," February 9, 1986
"Drug Testing Set for More Workers," September 3, 1986
"Drug Tests Promote Safety, Many Say," September 16, 1986
"FAA May Require Testing of Pilots for Use of Drugs," December 5, 1986
"Rockets Discuss Drug Temptation: Reaction to Banning," January 14, 1987
"Lloyd and Wiggins of Rockets Banned for Drug Use," January 14, 1987
"NCAA Testing Seen as Deterrent," January 14, 1987
"Post-Bowl Drug Testing Set," December 30, 1986
"Bosworth Tells of Steroid Use," December 26, 1986
"Amtrak Crash Spurs Call for Random Drug Tests," January 22, 1987
"Drug Trace Found in 2 Rail Workers After Fatal Crash," January 15, 1987

Time
"Putting Them All to the Test," October 21, 1985
"Drugs on the Job," March 17, 1986

US News & World Report
"Test Employees for Drug Use?" March 17, 1986

"Baseball's Drug Menace," March 17, 1986
"America on Drugs," July 28, 1986

The Wall Street Journal
"Too Many Bugs in Screening Measures," April 14, 1986

PROFESSIONAL JOURNALS:

The America Council for Drug Education
"Urine Testing in the Workplace," 1985

ACLU News
"ACLU Denounces Drug Testing Recommendations," March 4,
    1986

ABA Journal
"Drug Testing," February 1986
"Drugs at Work," March 1986
"Drug Test Limits," June 1986
"Mandatory Drug Testing," August 1986
"Protect Safety, Not Drug Abuse," August 1, 1986

The American Journal of Sports Medicine
"Anabolic Steroids in Athletics: How Well Do They Work and
    How Dangerous Are They?" 1984, vol. 12, no. 1.

Alcohol, Health and Research World
"Alcohol and Drug Abuse Among American Military Person-
    nel," Winter 85/86

Arbitration Journal
"Drug and Alcohol Issues in the Workplace," September 1984

California Lawyer
"Drug Testing Comes to Work," April 1986

Columbia Law Review
"Dragnet Drug Testing," May 1986

Criminal Justice Newsletter
"Organized Crime Panel Urges 'Suitable' Employee Drug
    Tests," March 17, 1986

Employee Relations Law Journal
"Drug and Alcohol Abuse in the Workplace," Fall 1985

Florida Bar Journal
"Drug Testing in the Workplace," June 1986

Journal of the American Medical Association
"Crisis in Drug Testing," April 26, 1985
"Laboratory Detection of Marijuana Use," August 9, 1985
"Cocaine in Herbal Tea," 1986

Journal of Drug Education
"Drug Abuse in the Military," 1983

Journal of Psychoactive Drugs
"Problems of Mass Urine Screening," October–December, 1984

National Law Journal
"Drug Testing: The Scene," April 1986

GOVERNMENT
PUBLICATIONS:

New York State Department of Substance Abuse Services
Handbook on Drug Abuse, 1978

National Institute on Alcohol Abuse and Alcoholism
Survey of Alcohol and Nonmedical Drug Use, 1985

National Institute on Drug Abuse
Drug Abuse and the American Adolescent, 1982
Drug Abuse Treatment Evaluation, 1985
Cocaine Use in America, April 1986
Drug Abuse in the Workplace, 1986
Drug Testing Federal Employees, 1986
Employee Drug Screening, 1986
Urine Testing for Drugs of Abuse, 1986

INDEX

-128